THE KINGFISHER
CHILDREN'S
ATLAS

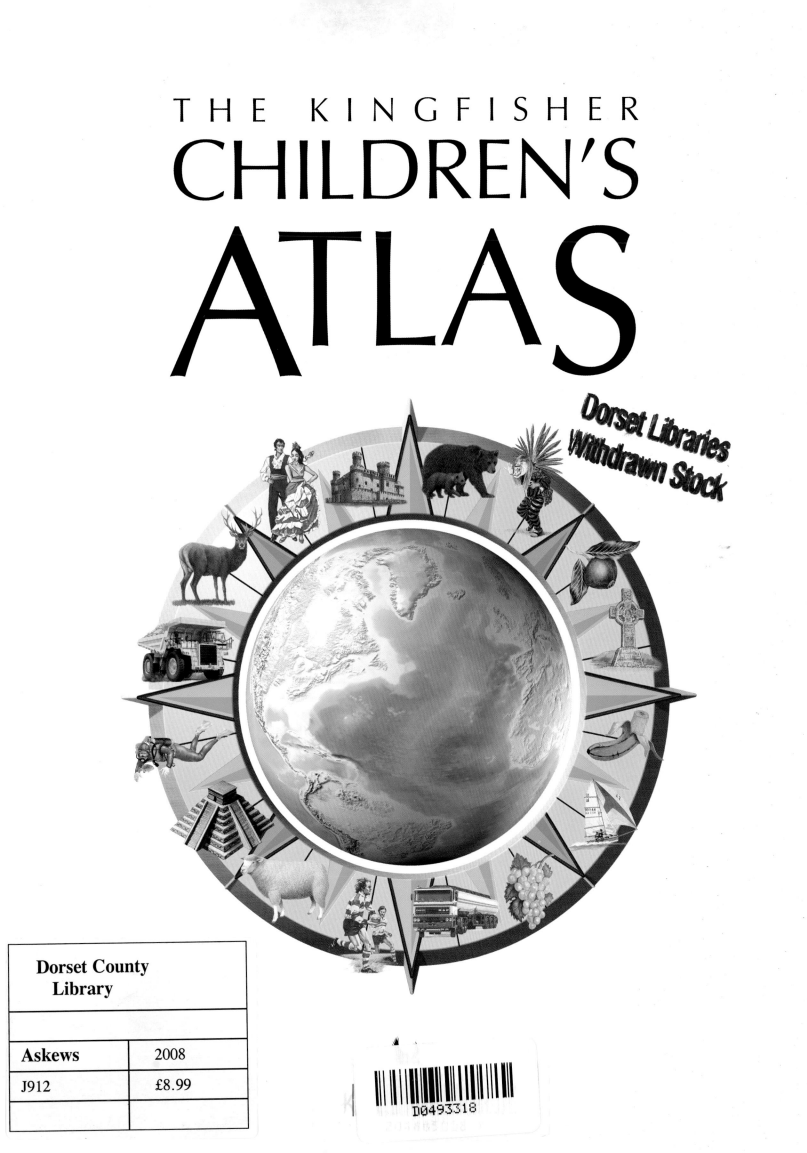

KINGFISHER

First published 2004 by Kingfisher

This edition published 2008 by Kingfisher
an imprint of Macmillan Children's Books
a division of Macmillan Publishers Limited
20 New Wharf Road, London N1 9RR
Basingstoke and Oxford
www.panmacmillan.com

Associated companies throughout the world

ISBN 978 0 7534 1707 2

Copyright © Macmillan Children's Books 2004

1 3 5 7 9 8 6 4 2
1TR/0108/SHENS/CLSN(CLSN)/158MA/F

A CIP catalogue record for this book is available from the British Library.

Printed in Taiwan

Written by
Belinda Weber

CONTENTS

THE EARTH

The Earth is a planet that rotates around the Sun. It is covered by huge land masses, called continents, and vast oceans and seas. There are seven continents: North America, South America, Europe, Africa, Asia, Australia and Antarctica. Most of them have a variety of different types of landscape. There are high, mountainous regions and low-lying plains. Where there is little or no rain, deserts are found. Flowing rivers can bring an abundance of animal and plant life to an area, and also cut paths through the landscape. In areas with high rainfall, rainforests can grow, providing lush green oases. Humans also influence the landscape. We farm the land and build villages, towns and huge cities with skyscrapers for people to live and work in.

Shaping the world

Humans also shape the landscape by dividing the land into countries. Some countries are whole islands, but most are parts of the larger land masses. Often, mountains or rivers mark the boundaries between countries, but sometimes there is nothing physical to mark the border where one country ends and another begins. Humans live on almost every bit of land on the planet. At present, there are around 6,600 million people living in the world.

Mountain ranges
Mountains reach high towards the sky. The higher they are, the colder the temperature. Very few animals can live at the tops.

Sandy deserts
In places with little or no rain, deserts, such as the Sahara, form. This sandy wilderness covers much of Northern Africa.

Winding rivers
Rivers and streams wind their way through the landscape on their way to the sea. They can carve paths through solid rock.

Green and wet
Tropical rainforests grow in hot, rainy areas, carpeting the land with a rich variety of plant life. Animals thrive in these forests.

Maps and mapping

We use maps and globes to show and find out about the countries of the world. A globe is a ball with all the continents and oceans drawn on it. A map is a flat plan of the world. Imagine that you had an orange with all the countries and seas drawn on it. If you peeled it and laid the peel out flat, you would not get a complete oblong. Map-makers make a whole picture by stretching the shape of some countries and seas. Map-makers also draw imaginary lines across the Earth's surface. Lines around the Earth are called lines of latitude. Lines going top to bottom are called lines of longitude. These form a grid over the Earth's surface, which help us pinpoint exactly where in the world a place is.

North Pole

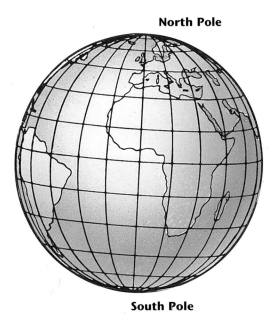

South Pole

Pole to pole
Lines going from top to bottom are called lines of longitude. All the lines of longitude meet at the North and South Poles, which are the most northerly and southerly points on Earth.

Greenwich meridian
The line of longitude in the middle of the Earth is called the Greenwich meridian.

Equator
Lines around the Earth are called lines of latitude. The equator is a line of latitude around the middle of the Earth.

Concrete jungles
Humans build huge cities to house millions of people. These urban buildings change the look of a once natural landscape.

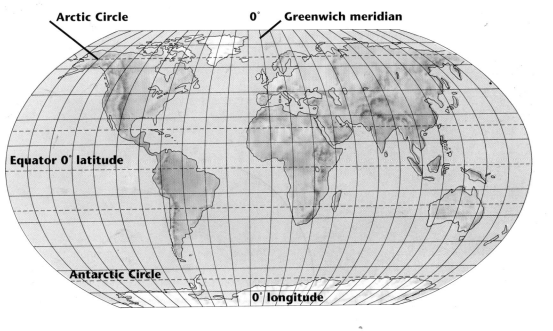

Arctic Circle

0°　Greenwich meridian

Equator 0° latitude

Antarctic Circle

0° longitude

Using maps

An atlas is a book of maps. Maps are pictures that tell us about different places. They provide all sorts of useful information about countries. Maps use different colours, symbols and lines to show mountains and valleys, oceans and seas, and rivers and lakes. On most of the maps in this atlas, like the example below, colours are also used to show the height of the land above sea level. Some maps use colours to show different kinds of information, such as where there are fertile places and deserts.

Red lines on the maps show where one country starts and another ends. These lines are called borders. Squares represent capital cities. A capital is the main city in a country, where the government and other important organizations are based. A few countries have more than one capital. All other towns and cities on the maps are marked with red dots. The maps in this atlas also have picture symbols which show you where to find animals, industry, landmarks and a variety of places of interest.

Aruba (to Netherlands)
Netherlands Antilles (to Netherlands)
GRENADA
Barranquilla
Maracaibo
Valencia
CARACAS
Isla de Margarita
TRINIDAD & TOBAGO
Iron ore mining
Maturín
Gulf of Darien
Lake Maracaibo
Barquisimeto
Apure
Orinoco
Embalse de Guri
GEORGETOWN
PARAMARIBO
Cúcuta
Oil
VENEZUELA
GUYANA
Cayenne
Medellín
Textiles
Magdalena
Llanos
Meta
Timber
Angel Falls
Guiana Highlands
Essequibo
SURINAME
French Guiana (to France)
Cauca
Oil
BOGOTÁ
Guaviare
Orinoco
Guiana Highlands
Emerald tree boa
Cali
COLOMBIA
Cocoa
Branco
Mouths of the Amazon
Viracocha stone statue
Coffee
Negro
Spider monkey
Represa de Balbina
Scarlet macaw
Isla de Marajó
Baía de Marajó
Equat
Caquetá
Amazon
Japurá
Piranha
Amazon
Belém
Napo
Putumayo
Basin
Manaus
Amazon
Tapajós
Iriri
Represa Tucuruí
Baía
Cattle
Hoatzin
Marañón
Toucan
Amazon
Rainforest
Sloth
Ucayali
BRAZIL
Xingu
Jurua
Madeira
Purus
São Manuel
Parnaíba
Copper mining
Brazil nuts
Logging
Madre de Dios
Juruena
Araguaia
Tocantins
Represa de Sobradinho
Huascarán 6,768 m
PERU
LIMA
Machu Picchu

The maps in this atlas use a set group of symbols and words to mark various different types of features. This key shows you what they all mean.

Settlements

■ CARACAS   Capital city
■ Denver   State capital city
● Manaus   Major city or town
• Maturín   Other city or town

Political and cultural regions

BRAZIL   Country

Aruba   Dependent territory
(to Netherlands)

ARIZONA   State, province or national region

Boundaries

〰〰   International border
• • •   Disputed border
– – –   State, province or national regional boundary

Drainage features

〰〰   River
- - -   Seasonal river
⌂⌂⌂   Canal
⌐＿   Waterfall
◯   Lake
⌐ - ⌐   Seasonal lake

Topographic features

△ *Cotopaxi 5,897 m*   Height of mountain
Isla de Marájo   Island / island group
Amazon Basin   Physical feature / landscape region

Seas and oceans

PACIFIC OCEAN   Name of ocean
Caribbean Sea   Name of sea

    Sea

Ice features

◁◁◁◁   Limit of summer pack ice
〰〰   Limit of winter pack ice

Land height

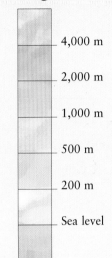

4,000 m
2,000 m
1,000 m
500 m
200 m
Sea level

Extra information

Alongside the maps, you will find symbols telling you more about the area covered by the map, to help you understand where it fits in the world.

Flags

Every country in the world has its own national flag. You will find these flags throughout the atlas. They symbolize the country's independence and identity.

Globe

The globe on each page shows (marked in orange) where the countries on the map are in the world. Some of the map pages have an extra map in a small box, called an inset. The position of these is shown by an orange box on the globe.

Scale bar

All the maps in this atlas have a scale bar. This will tell you how distances on the page relate to real distances on the ground. For example, the scale bar shown below tells you that 28 mm on the map represents 500 km on the ground.

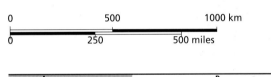

0   500   1000 km
0   250   500 miles

A   B

Grid

Around the edges of each page you will find a grid with letters and numbers. The index at the end of the book will give you a page number and grid reference. By using the grid reference, you will be able to find the particular town or city you are looking for.

Picture symbols

On the maps, you will also find picture symbols which show interesting features in each country. Here are a few examples. Look out for more throughout the atlas.

Industry
Fortaleza

Cabo de São Roque

Coffee

Natal

Recife

Sugar cane

Catedral Basílica

Cattle
An example of a farm animal

Fishing
An example of a type of industry

Toucan
An example of a kind of wildlife

Catedral Basílica
An example of a famous building or landmark

Bananas
An example of a food crop

Countries of the world

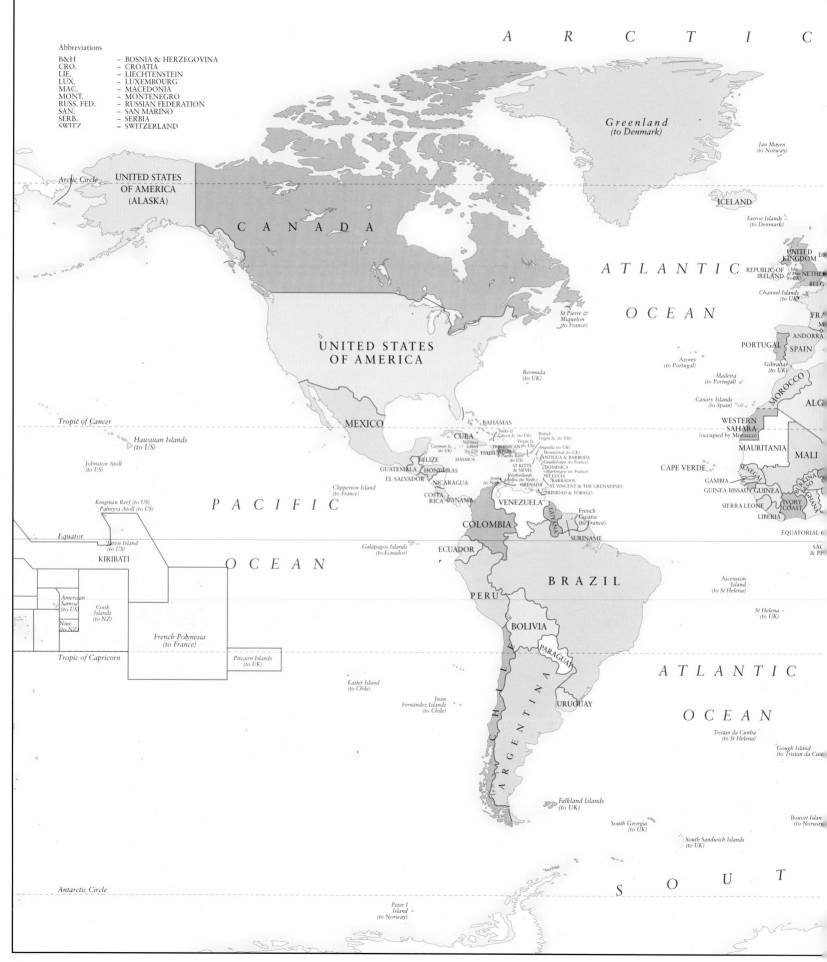

A R C T I C

Greenland
(to Denmark)

Jan Mayen
(to Norway)

Arctic Circle

UNITED STATES
OF AMERICA
(ALASKA)

ICELAND

Faeroe Islands
(to Denmark)

C A N A D A

A T L A N T I C

UNITED
KINGDOM

REPUBLIC OF
IRELAND

Isle of Man
(to UK)

NETHER

BELG

St Pierre &
Miquelon
(to France)

O C E A N

Channel Islands
(to UK)

FRA

M

UNITED STATES
OF AMERICA

ANDORRA

Bermuda
(to UK)

PORTUGAL   SPAIN

Azores
(to Portugal)

Gibraltar
(to UK)

Madeira
(to Portugal)

MOROCCO

Tropic of Cancer

Canary Islands
(to Spain)

ALG

Hawaiian Islands
(to US)

MEXICO

BAHAMAS

WESTERN
SAHARA
(occupied by Morocco)

CUBA

Turks &
Caicos Is. (to UK)

MAURITANIA

MALI

Johnston Atoll
(to US)

Navassa
Island
(to US)

Cayman Is.
(to UK)

Virgin Is.
(to US)

British
Virgin Is. (to UK)

Anguilla (to UK)

Montserrat (to UK)

CAPE VERDE

DOMINICAN
REPUBLIC

BELIZE

JAMAICA

HAITI   Puerto Rico
(to US)

ANTIGUA & BARBUDA

ST KITTS
& NEVIS

Guadeloupe (to France)

DOMINICA

GUATEMALA

HONDURAS

ST LUCIA
Martinique (to France)

SENEGAL

GAMBIA

GUINEA-BISSAU   GUINEA

BURKINA

GHANA

EL SALVADOR

NICARAGUA

Netherlands
Antilles (to Neth.)

BARBADOS

ST VINCENT & THE GRENADINES

GRENADA

SIERRA LEONE

IVORY
COAST

Kingman Reef (to US)

Palmyra Atoll (to US)

COSTA
RICA   PANAMA

Aruba
(to Neth.)

TRINIDAD & TOBAGO

LIBERIA

P A C I F I C

Clipperton Island
(to France)

VENEZUELA

French
Guiana
(to France)

EQUATORIAL G

Equator

Jarvis Island
(to US)

COLOMBIA

GUYANA

SURINAME

SÃO
& PR

KIRIBATI

O C E A N

Galapagos Islands
(to Ecuador)

ECUADOR

Ascension
Island
(to St Helena)

American
Samoa
(to US)

Cook
Islands
(to NZ)

B R A Z I L

PERU

Niue
(to NZ)

St Helena
(to UK)

French Polynesia
(to France)

BOLIVIA

Tropic of Capricorn

Pitcairn Islands
(to UK)

PARAGUAY

A T L A N T I C

Easter Island
(to Chile)

Juan
Fernández Islands
(to Chile)

CHILE

ARGENTINA

URUGUAY

O C E A N

Tristan da Cunha
(to St Helena)

Gough Island
(to Tristan da Cun

Falkland Islands
(to UK)

South Georgia
(to UK)

Bouvet Islan
(to Norway)

South Sandwich Islands
(to UK)

Antarctic Circle

S O U T

Peter I
Island
(to Norway)

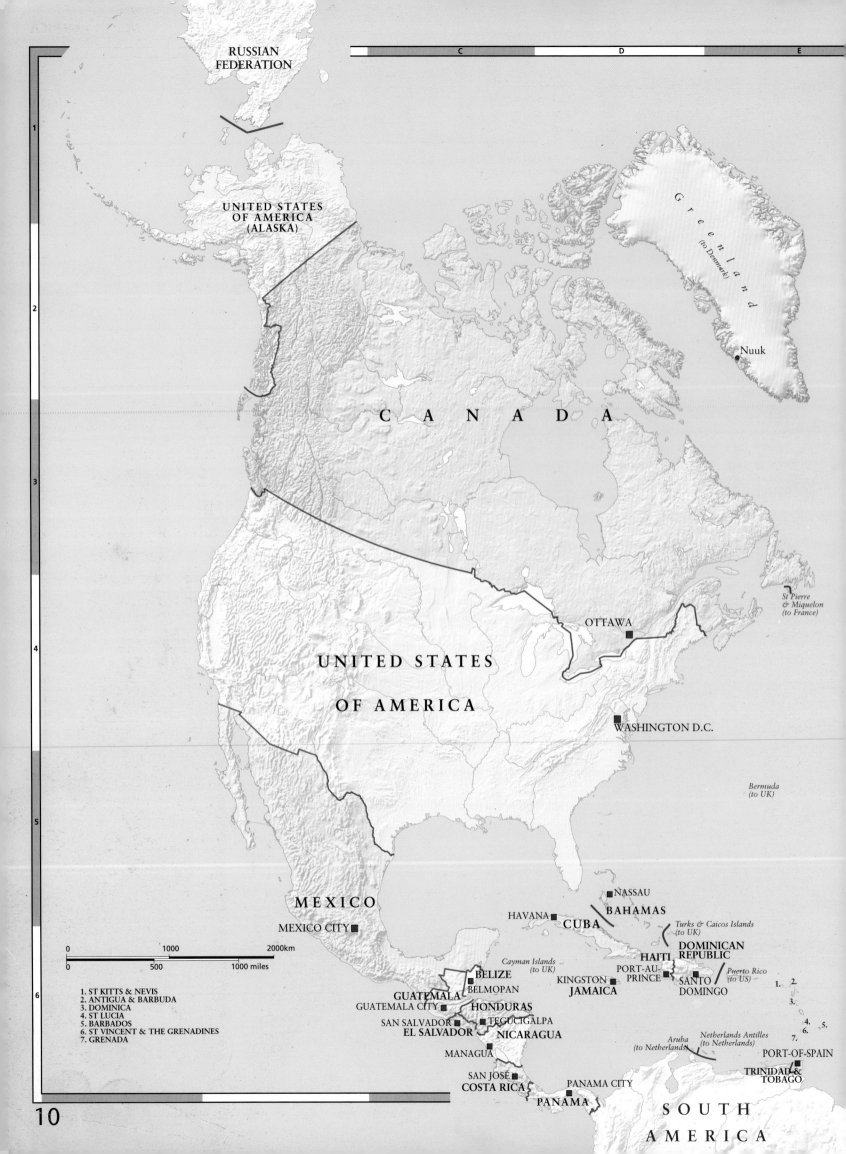

RUSSIAN
FEDERATION

UNITED STATES
OF AMERICA
(ALASKA)

Greenland
(to Denmark)

Nuuk

C A N A D A

OTTAWA

St Pierre
& Miquelon
(to France)

UNITED STATES

OF AMERICA

WASHINGTON D.C.

Bermuda
(to UK)

MEXICO

NASSAU

HAVANA   CUBA   BAHAMAS

Turks & Caicos Islands
(to UK)

MEXICO CITY

1000   2000km

0   500   1000 miles

Cayman Islands
(to UK)

DOMINICAN
REPUBLIC

HAITI

Puerto Rico
(to US)

1.   2.

PORT-AU-
PRINCE

3.

KINGSTON
JAMAICA

SANTO
DOMINGO

BELIZE

1. ST KITTS & NEVIS
2. ANTIGUA & BARBUDA
3. DOMINICA
4. ST LUCIA
5. BARBADOS
6. ST VINCENT & THE GRENADINES
7. GRENADA

BELMOPAN

4.

GUATEMALA

6.

5.

GUATEMALA CITY   HONDURAS

SAN SALVADOR   TEGUCIGALPA

7.

EL SALVADOR   NICARAGUA

Aruba
(to Netherlands)

Netherlands Antilles
(to Netherlands)

MANAGUA

PORT-OF-SPAIN

SAN JOSÉ
COSTA RICA   PANAMA CITY   TRINIDAD &
TOBAGO

PANAMA   S O U T H

A M E R I C A

10

Rich farmland
The Mississippi river carries sediment (tiny specks of mud) in its waters which it leaves as fertile soil along its way. Many crops are grown on the plains beside the river.

NORTH AMERICA

The continent of North America is the third largest continent. It stretches from the frozen Arctic in the north to the tropics in the south. In winter, the far north is bitterly cold as icy winds blow off the Arctic. Most parts of the continent have warm or hot summers. The Rocky Mountains stretch down the west of the continent, reaching from the north of Canada to Mexico. On the east of the continent lie the Appalachians, and in between these two mountain ranges are large flat plains, across which the mighty Mississippi and Missouri rivers flow.

North America consists of three large countries: Canada, the United States of America and Mexico; as well as the island of Greenland and the smaller countries of Central America and the Caribbean.

Crystal clear
Canada has more lakes and inland water than anywhere else in the world. Many national parks have been set up to protect the lakes and the areas surrounding them.

Thumbs up!
People from many different cultures make up the United States of America. Settlers from Europe, Africa and Asia as well as the native Americans are all part of a multicultural society.

Canada

Canada is an enormous country – the second largest in the world after the Russian Federation. Yet most of Canada's 30 million people live in the south, in cities along the border with the United States. Very few people live in the Northwest Territories, or in the islands off the north, as the lands here are inside the Arctic Circle and temperatures can drop to a bitterly cold -40°C. The Rocky Mountains in the west are covered with trees, and are home to wildlife such as the bald eagle. In the far north, there are polar bears. In the central areas are vast plains, where large quantities of wheat are grown.

Half of Canada's population live along the St Lawrence Seaway, near the Great Lakes. Canada has two official languages – French and English. Most of the French-speaking Canadians live in the province of Québec.

Long journey
Monarch butterflies from Canada gather in their thousands each autumn and fly south. They spend the winter in Florida, southern California and northern Mexico. Some travel over 3,430 km.

FACTS AND FIGURES

Largest cities
Toronto 5,113,000
Montreal 3,636,000

Longest river
Mackenzie-Peace 4,241 km

Largest lake
Lake Superior 82,350 km². This is the largest lake in North America and the second largest in the world

Highest mountain
Mount Logan 5,959 m

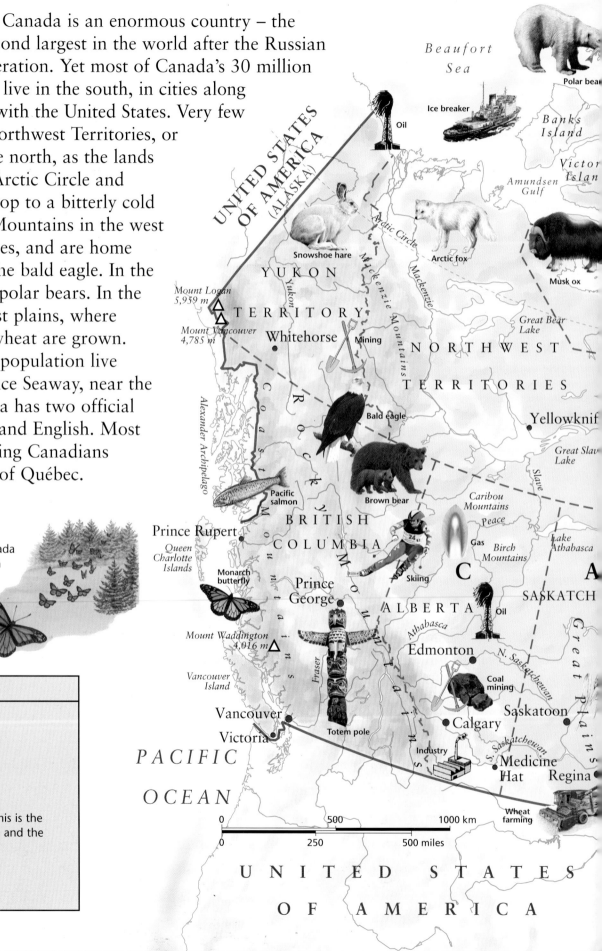

ARCTIC OCEAN

Beaufort Sea

Polar bear

Ice breaker

Banks Island

Victoria Island

Amundsen Gulf

Oil

UNITED STATES OF AMERICA (ALASKA)

Arctic Circle

Snowshoe hare

Arctic fox

YUKON

Mackenzie

Mackenzie Mountains

Great Bear Lake

Mount Logan 5,959 m

Mount Vancouver 4,785 m

TERRITORY

Whitehorse

Mining

NORTHWEST

Yukon

TERRITORIES

Yellowknif

Great Slav Lake

Musk ox

Coast Mountains

Bald eagle

Alexander Archipelago

Slave

Prince Rupert

Pacific salmon

Brown bear

Caribou Mountains

Peace

Lake Athabasca

Queen Charlotte Islands

BRITISH COLUMBIA

Rocky Mountains

Gas

Birch Mountains

C

A

Skiing

SASKATCH

Monarch butterfly

Prince George

ALBERTA

Oil

Mount Waddington 4,016 m

Fraser

Athabasca

Edmonton

N. Saskatchewan

Great Plains

Vancouver Island

Coal mining

Totem pole

Calgary

Saskatoon

Vancouver

Victoria

S. Saskatchewan

PACIFIC

Industry

Medicine Hat

Regina

OCEAN

Wheat farming

UNITED STATES OF AMERICA

0   500   1000 km
0   250   500 miles

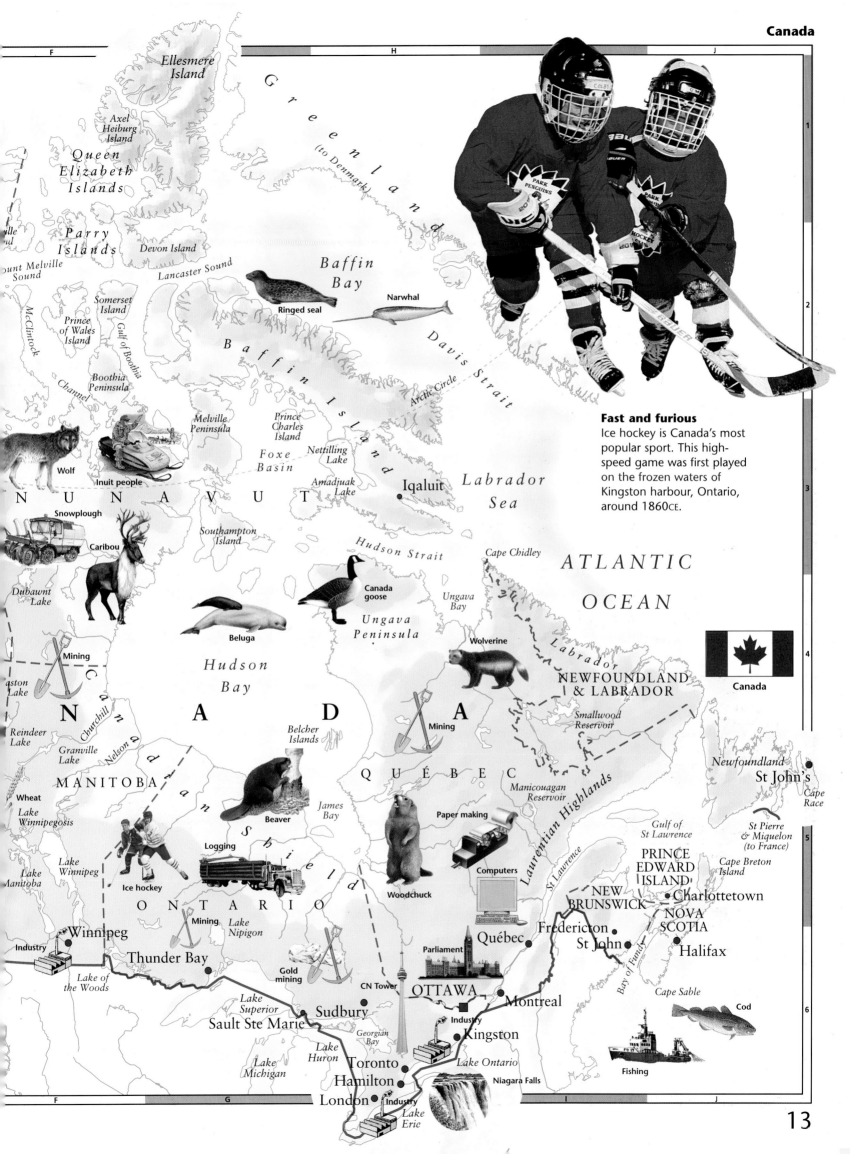

Ellesmere Island

Axel Heiberg Island

Queen Elizabeth Islands

Parry Islands

Devon Island

Greenland (to Denmark)

Lancaster Sound

Mount Melville Sound

Somerset Island

Prince of Wales Island

Gulf of Boothia

Boothia Peninsula

Channel

McClintock

Baffin Bay

Ringed seal

Narwhal

Davis Strait

Melville Peninsula

Prince Charles Island

Baffin Island

Foxe Basin

Nettilling Lake

Amadjuak Lake

Iqaluit

Labrador Sea

Arctic Circle

Wolf

Inuit people

Snowplough

Caribou

Dubawnt Lake

NUNAVUT

Southampton Island

Hudson Strait

Cape Chidley

ATLANTIC OCEAN

Ungava Bay

Canada goose

Ungava Peninsula

Beluga

Belcher Islands

Hudson Bay

Mining

aston Lake

Reindeer Lake

Granville Lake

Churchill

Nelson

Wolverine

Labrador

NEWFOUNDLAND & LABRADOR

Canada

MANITOBA

C a n a d i a n   S h i e l d

James Bay

QUÉBEC

Smallwood Reservoir

Manicouagan Reservoir

Laurentian Highlands

Newfoundland

St John's

Cape Race

Mining

Beaver

Logging

Wheat

Lake Winnipegosis

Lake Winnipeg

Lake Manitoba

Ice hockey

ONTARIO

Mining

Lake Nipigon

Woodchuck

Paper making

Computers

St Pierre & Miquelon (to France)

Gulf of St Lawrence

Cape Breton Island

PRINCE EDWARD ISLAND

NEW BRUNSWICK

Charlottetown

NOVA SCOTIA

Industry

Winnipeg

Thunder Bay

Lake of the Woods

Gold mining

CN Tower

Parliament

Québec

St Lawrence

Fredericton

St John

Halifax

Bay of Fundy

Cape Sable

Cod

OTTAWA

Montreal

Lake Superior

Sudbury

Sault Ste Marie

Georgian Bay

Lake Huron

Industry

Kingston

Lake Ontario

Fishing

Toronto

Hamilton

Lake Michigan

London

Industry

Lake Erie

Niagara Falls

Fast and furious

Ice hockey is Canada's most popular sport. This high-speed game was first played on the frozen waters of Kingston harbour, Ontario, around 1860CE.

Western United States

The United States of America occupies the central part of the continent of North America. This powerful country is divided into 50 states. The land and climate across such a huge country varies greatly, from icy Arctic wilderness in Alaska to burning hot deserts in Arizona, swamps in the Everglades, and rolling grasslands in the prairies of the mid-west.

The western USA includes landmarks such as the Grand Canyon, a deep gorge carved out by the Colorado river. In California, the climate is perfect for orange-growing. It is also the home of Silicon Valley, where microchips and electronic devices are produced.

Strait of Juan de Fuca
Cape Flattery
Aircraft manufacturing
Mount Olympus 2,428 m
Seattle
WASHINGTON
Olympia
Spokane
Columbia
Mount Rainier 4,392 m
Apples
Columbia Basin
Mount Saint Helens 2,549 m
Snake
Portland
Columbia
Clearwater Mountains
Salem
IDAHO
Fishing
Eugene
Sheep
Salmon River Mountains
Timber production
OREGON
Potato
Golden eagle
Malheur Lake
Boise
Columbia Plateau
Giant redwood
Blue Mountains
Snake
Cape Mendocino
Coast Ranges
Pit
Brown bear
Gold mining
Humboldt
U N
Mount Shasta 4,316 m
Wine
Pyramid Lake
Great Salt Lake
Sacramento
Gold mining
Great Salt Lake Desert
Golden Gate Bridge
Reno
Kit fox
Lake Tahoe
Carson City
Great
San Francisco
Sacramento
NEVADA
Sevier Lake
San Jose
Electronics (Silicon Valley)
Grapes
Basin
Co
Monterey Bay
Casinos
Fresno
Mount Whitney 4,418 m
Rattlesnake
CALIFORNIA
Sierra Nevada
Death Valley
Sealion
Las Vegas
Lake Mead
Grand Canyon
Pl
Point Conception
Oranges
Mojave Desert
Hoover Dam
Grand Canyon
Hollywood
Los Angeles
Desert tortoise
ARIZON
Colorado
PACIFIC
Phoenix
San Diego
Salton Sea
Gila
OCEAN
Sonoran Desert
Tucs
Gila monster

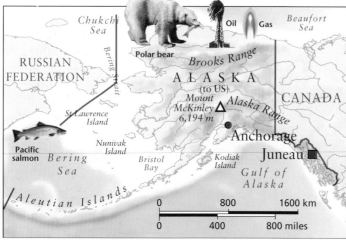

Chukchi Sea
Oil
Gas
Beaufort Sea
Polar bear
RUSSIAN FEDERATION
Bering Strait
Brooks Range
ALASKA (to US)
St Lawrence Island
Mount McKinley 6,194 m
Alaska Range
CANADA
Nunivak Island
Pacific salmon
Bering Sea
Bristol Bay
Kodiak Island
Anchorage
Juneau
Gulf of Alaska
Aleutian Islands

| 0 | 800 | 1600 km |
| 0 | 400 | 800 miles |

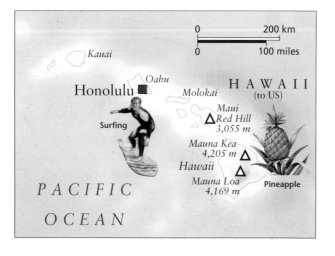

| 0 | 200 km |
| 0 | 100 miles |

Kauai
Oahu
Honolulu
Molokai
HAWAII (to US)
Surfing
Maui
Red Hill 3,055 m
Mauna Kea 4,205 m
Hawaii
Mauna Loa 4,169 m
Pineapple
PACIFIC OCEAN

FACTS AND FIGURES

Largest cities
Los Angeles 12,950,000
Dallas 6,004,000

Largest state
Alaska

Longest river
Mississippi-Missouri 6,020 km

Highest mountain
Mount McKinley 6,194 m

Lowest point
Death Valley 86 m below sea level

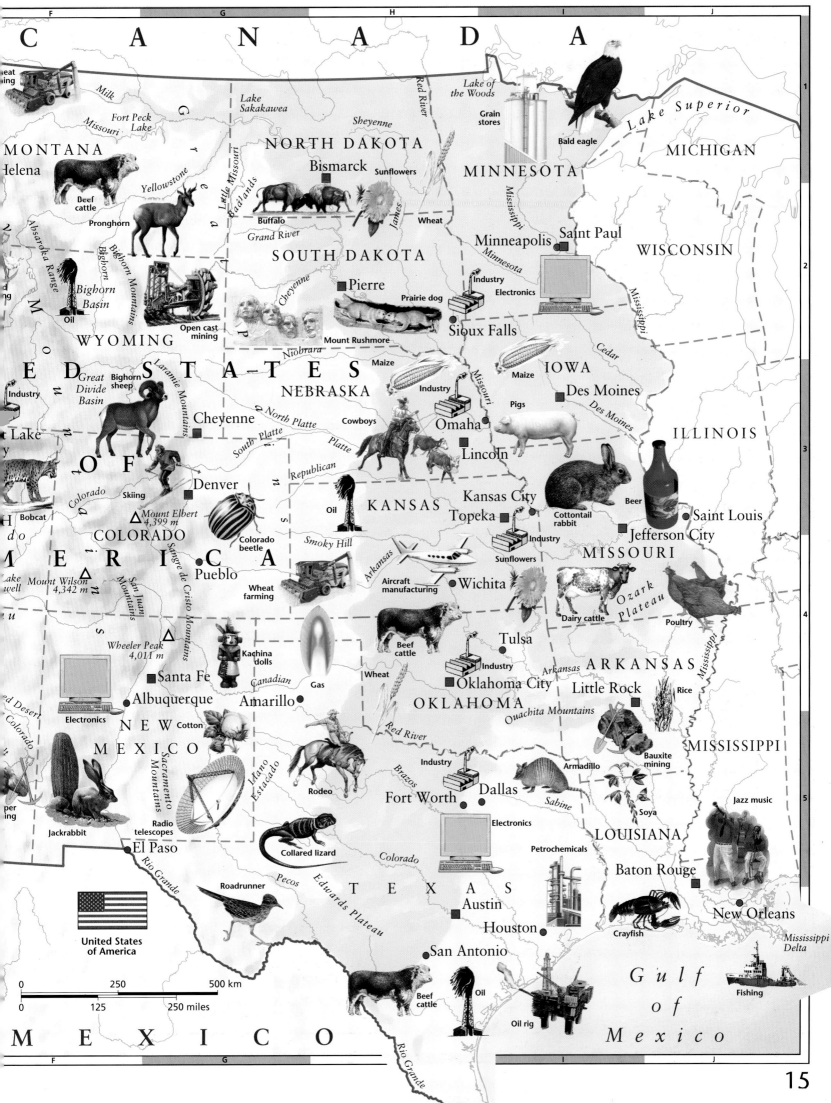

C A N A D A

MONTANA
Helena
Beef cattle
Pronghorn
Milk
Missouri
Fort Peck Lake
Yellowstone

Absaroka Range

Oil
Bighorn Basin
Bighorn Mountains
Open cast mining
WYOMING

Great Divide Basin
Bighorn sheep
Laramie Mountains

Industry

Lake

Bobcat

Skiing
Denver
Mount Elbert 4,399 m
COLORADO
Colorado beetle
Pueblo
Mount Wilson 4,342 m
San Juan Mountains
Sangre de Cristo Mountains

Colorado

Wheeler Peak 4,011 m
Santa Fe
Albuquerque
Electronics
NEW MEXICO
Kachina dolls
Sacramento Mountains
Cotton

Jackrabbit
Radio telescopes

El Paso
Rio Grande

United States of America

Roadrunner
Pecos
Rio Grande

Collared lizard

Edwards Plateau

Llano Estacado
Rodeo
Amarillo
Gas

T E X A S
Austin
Houston
San Antonio
Beef cattle
Oil
Oil rig

Little Missouri
Lake Sakakawea
NORTH DAKOTA
Bismarck
Badlands
Buffalo
Grand River
Sunflowers
Sheyenne
Red River

Cheyenne
SOUTH DAKOTA
Pierre
Mount Rushmore
Niobrara
Prairie dog

Maize
NEBRASKA
Cheyenne
North Platte
South Platte
Platte
Republican
Cowboys
Omaha
Lincoln
Oil
KANSAS
Smoky Hill
Arkansas
Wheat farming
Aircraft manufacturing
Wichita
Sunflowers
Wheat

Red River
Canadian
OKLAHOMA
Oklahoma City
Tulsa
Beef cattle
Industry
Wheat
Brazos
Industry
Fort Worth
Dallas
Electronics
Colorado
Sabine
Armadillo

Lake of the Woods
Grain stores
Bald eagle

MINNESOTA
Mississippi
Minnesota
Minneapolis
Saint Paul
Wheat
Industry
Electronics
Sioux Falls

Maize
Industry
Missouri
IOWA
Maize
Pigs
Des Moines
Des Moines
Cedar

Kansas City
Topeka
Cottontail rabbit
Industry
MISSOURI
Dairy cattle
Ozark Plateau
Poultry

Beer
Saint Louis
Jefferson City

ARKANSAS
Little Rock
Ouachita Mountains
Rice
Bauxite mining

MISSISSIPPI

Soya
LOUISIANA
Petrochemicals
Baton Rouge
Crayfish
New Orleans

Jazz music
Mississippi Delta
Fishing

G u l f   o f   M e x i c o

Crayfish

MICHIGAN
Lake Superior
WISCONSIN
Mississippi
ILLINOIS
Rabbit

M E X I C O

Scale:
0   250   500 km
0   125   250 miles

U N I T E D   S T A T E S   O F   A M E R I C A

15

Eastern United States

The eastern parts of the USA were home to the first European settlers who arrived in America in the 17th century CE, and they remain the most densely populated areas today. They contain major cities such as New York, Chicago and Washington D.C. Stretching from the rocky shores of Maine down to the sunny islands of Florida Keys, the eastern seaboard (coast) has a varied landscape with many bays and inlets. Further inland, the Appalachian mountain system, which is rich in mineral deposits, cuts through the country. Much of the surrounding area is still covered in trees – in West Virginia, for example, 75 per cent of the land is forest. The states surrounding the Gulf of Mexico enjoy a mostly temperate climate.

Florida is warm all year round. It is popular with tourists from the USA and around the world, and is also home to the Kennedy Space Center at Cape Canaveral.

The White House
Situated in Washington D.C. (District of Columbia), the White House is the official home of the President of the United States of America. Washington D.C. is the capital of the USA.

Basketball

Basketball is the only major sport to have been invented in the USA. It was invented in 1891ce and involves two teams of five players trying to score by tossing a ball through the opponent's hoop and net, which is called a basket!

FACTS AND FIGURES

Largest cities
New York 18,819,000
Chicago 9,506,000
Philadelphia 5,827,000

Largest lake
Lake Superior 82,350 km²

Highest mountain
Mount Washington 1,917 m

United States of America

Swordfish

DELAWARE
MARYLAND
Annapolis
WASHINGTON D.C.
The White House
Chesapeake Bay
VIRGINIA
Richmond
Norfolk
Tobacco
Cape Hatteras
Opossum
Eggs
Cape Fear
Poultry
NORTH CAROLINA
Raleigh
Machinery
WEST VIRGINIA
Charleston
Allegheny Mountains
Charlotte
SOUTH CAROLINA
Columbia
Charleston
Textiles
Tobacco
Savannah
ATLANTIC
Savannah
OCEAN
OHIO
Cincinnati
Thoroughbred horse
Ohio
Coal mining
Mount Rogers 1,746 m
Blue Ridge
Appalachian Mountains
Piedmont
Skunk
GEORGIA
Peaches
Peanut farming
Cape Canaveral launch site
Cape Canaveral
Brown pelican
UNITED STATES
KENTUCKY
Frankfort
Louisville
Wright brothers
INDIANA
Maize
Soya
ILLINOIS
Wabash
Springfield
Mississippi
MISSOURI
Country music
Nashville
TENNESSEE
Chattanooga
Tennessee
OF
AMERICA
Atlanta
Chattahoochee
ALABAMA
Birmingham
Cotton
Steel making
Montgomery
Alabama
Raccoon
Tallahassee
FLORIDA
Jacksonville
Orlando
Epcot Center
Oranges
Tampa
Lake Okeechobee
The Everglades
Alligator
Fort Lauderdale
Miami
Tourism
Florida Keys
Cape Sable
BAHAMAS
ARKANSAS
Memphis
Cotton
Catfish
MISSISSIPPI
Jackson
Cotton
Steamboat
Tombigbee
Mississippi
Mississippi Delta
LOUISIANA
Mobile
Cargo ship
Cape San Blas
Gulf Coastal Plain
Gulf of Mexico

400 km
200 miles
200
100
0
0

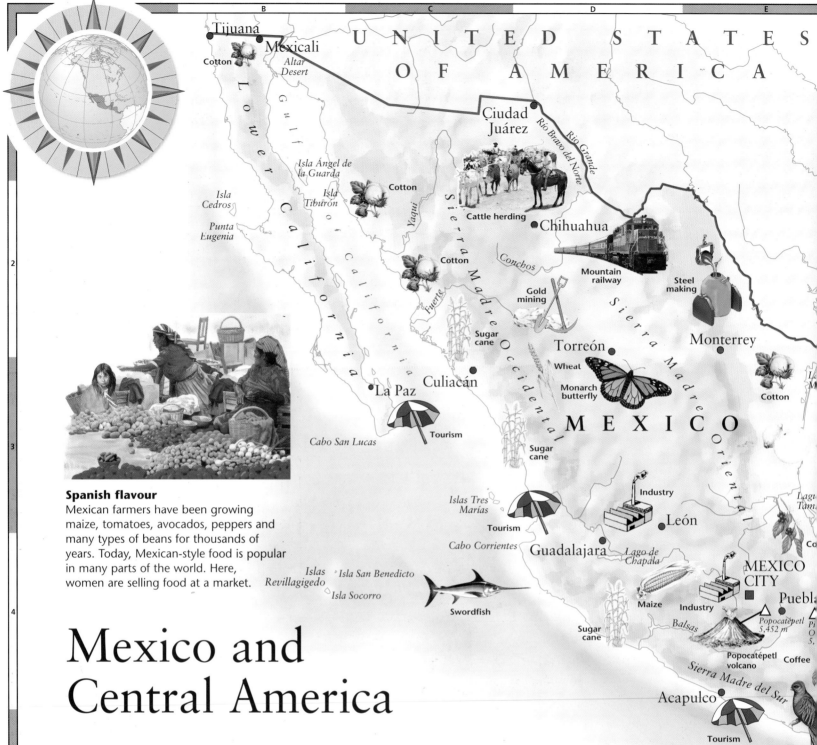

Spanish flavour
Mexican farmers have been growing maize, tomatoes, avocados, peppers and many types of beans for thousands of years. Today, Mexican-style food is popular in many parts of the world. Here, women are selling food at a market.

Mexico and Central America

Mexico and Central America make up a land bridge that links the USA to South America. Mexico is a country of deserts, volcanoes and tropical forests. Further south lie Guatemala, Belize, Honduras, El Salvador, Nicaragua, Costa Rica and Panama. The region's lush rainforests are home to many animals, including monkeys, butterflies and brightly coloured macaws and quetzals. Long ago, Aztec, Maya and Olmec civilizations thrived in Mexico and Central America.

The Panama Canal, the busiest big-ship canal in the world, is in Panama. It is 82 km long and links the Pacific and Atlantic oceans. Before it opened in 1914CE, ships had to travel all the way around South America to reach the other ocean.

Going bananas
Bananas are the main crop in Honduras. They account for almost a quarter of the country's income.

Bustling city
Mexico City is the third largest city in the world and home to more than 19 million inhabitants. People enjoy watching bull fighting, or sports such as baseball or football, at these large stadiums.

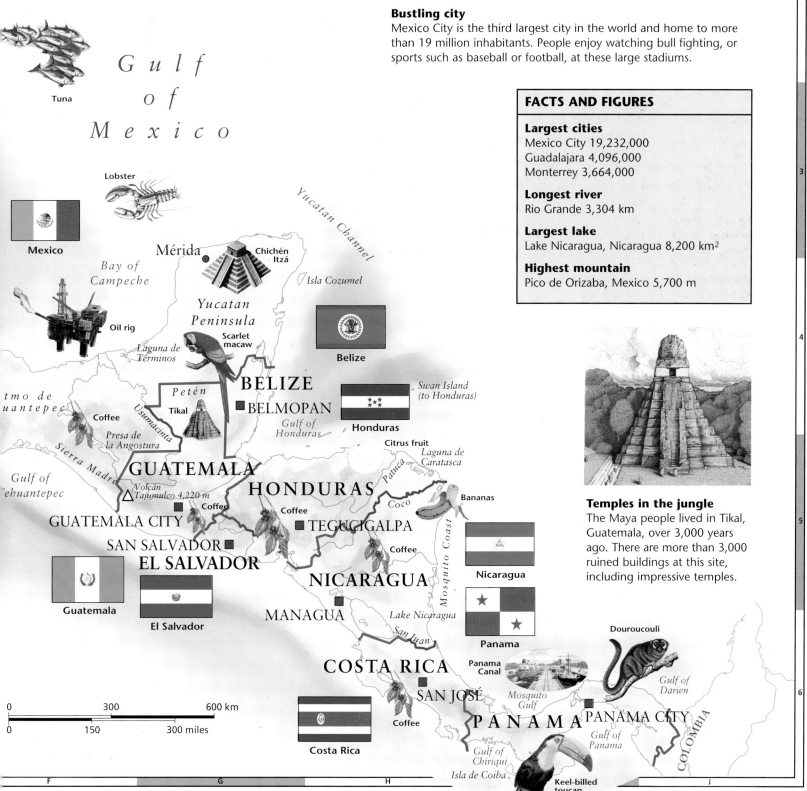

Tuna

Gulf
of
Mexico

Lobster

Mexico

Bay of Campeche

Mérida

Chichén Itzá

Yucatan Channel

Isla Cozumel

Yucatan Peninsula

Oil rig

Scarlet macaw

Laguna de Términos

BELIZE

BELMOPAN

Swan Island (to Honduras)

Belize

Honduras

Coffee

Petén

Tikal

Usumacinta

Gulf of Honduras

Citrus fruit

Laguna de Caratasca

Istmo de Tehuantepec

Presa de la Angostura

GUATEMALA

Sierra Madre

Patuca

HONDURAS

Coco

Bananas

Gulf of Tehuantepec

△ *Volcán Tajumulco 4,220 m*

Coffee

Coffee

TEGUCIGALPA

Coffee

Mosquito Coast

GUATEMALA CITY

SAN SALVADOR

Coffee

NICARAGUA

Nicaragua

EL SALVADOR

Guatemala

El Salvador

MANAGUA

Lake Nicaragua

San Juan

Panama

COSTA RICA

Panama Canal

Mosquito Gulf

Dourocouli

Gulf of Darien

SAN JOSÉ

PANAMA CITY

Coffee

PANAMA

Gulf of Panama

Costa Rica

Gulf of Chiriquí
Isla de Coiba

COLOMBIA

Keel-billed toucan

0	300	600 km
0	150	300 miles

FACTS AND FIGURES

Largest cities
Mexico City 19,232,000
Guadalajara 4,096,000
Monterrey 3,664,000

Longest river
Rio Grande 3,304 km

Largest lake
Lake Nicaragua, Nicaragua 8,200 km²

Highest mountain
Pico de Orizaba, Mexico 5,700 m

Temples in the jungle
The Maya people lived in Tikal, Guatemala, over 3,000 years ago. There are more than 3,000 ruined buildings at this site, including impressive temples.

UNITED STATES
OF AMERICA
(FLORIDA)

*Gulf of
Mexico*

Tourism

*Grand
Bahama Island* ·Freeport

*Great
Abaco*

Bahamas

*Eleuthera
Island*

NASSAU
*New
Providence*

*Cat
Island*

BAHAMAS

*Long
Island*

Cuba

Straits of Florida

HAVANA

Tobacco

CUBA

Fishing

*Acklin
Island*

Cigar making

*Isla de la
Juventud*

Sugar
cane

·Camagüey

G

r

Scuba diving

e

a

Cutting
sugar cane

t

Santiago
de Cuba

*Cayman
Islands
(to UK)*

*Grand
Cayman*

e

Tourism

r

Montego Bay

JAMAICA

*Navassa Island
(to US)*

Bananas

Mining

KINGSTON

Cruise liner

Jamaica

Party time!
Festivals and carnivals are a time to party.
People wear colourful costumes and play
music as they parade through the streets.

The Caribbean

A string of islands separates the Atlantic Ocean from the
Caribbean Sea. There are many different countries in the
Caribbean and hundreds of islands. Cuba is the largest island,
stretching over 1,100 km in length. Haiti and the Dominican
Republic share ownership of the second biggest island,
Hispaniola. Some of the other islands are so small that
no one lives on them. All the islands enjoy a tropical climate
with a rainy season between June and November.
Occasionally, violent storms, called hurricanes, sweep through
the Caribbean. The strong winds and torrential rain can cause
serious damage. Coral reefs surround many of the islands,
and holidaymakers can scuba dive in the warm waters or
explore the islands' many beautiful palm-fringed beaches.

FACTS AND FIGURES

Largest cities
Santo Domingo 2,930,000
Havana 2,202,000
Port-au-Prince 1,977,000

Highest point
Pico Duarte 3,175 m

Number of islands
Over 100

Number of hurricanes
6 per year on average, in the hurricane
season between June and November,
reaching up to 250 km/h

Beach paradise
Holidaymakers flock to the Caribbean to enjoy the white, sandy beaches. The money they spend there is vital for the countries' economies.

ATLANTIC OCEAN

West Indies

Turks & Caicos Islands
(to UK)

Great Inagua

Port-de-Paix

Santiago

DOMINICAN REPUBLIC

Leeward Islands

Puerto Rico
(to US)

British Virgin Islands
(to UK)

Anguilla
(to UK)

HAITI

Pico Duarte
3,175 m

Hispaniola

San Juan

Virgin Islands
(to US)

St Martin
(to France & Netherlands)

St Barthélémy (to France)

PORT-AU-PRINCE

Cocoa

SANTO DOMINGO

Mona Passage

Netherlands Antilles
(to Netherlands)

Barbuda

St Kitts

ANTIGUA & BARBUDA

Nevis

ST JOHN'S

BASSETERRE

Antigua

ST KITTS & NEVIS

Guadeloupe Passage

Grande Terre

Montserrat
(to UK)

Basse Terre

Guadeloupe
(to France)

Antilles

Haiti

Dominican Republic

St Kitts & Nevis

Guadeloupe Passage

Basse Terre

Antigua & Barbuda

Caribbean Sea

DOMINICA

ROSEAU

Martinique Passage

Dominica

Martinique
(to France)

Fort-de-France

ST LUCIA

Barbados

Shark

St Lucia

Sailing

CASTRIES

St Vincent Passage

BARBADOS

KINGSTOWN

St Vincent

BRIDGETOWN

Lesser

Aruba
(to Netherlands)

Netherlands Antilles
(to Netherlands)

Oranjestad

ST VINCENT & THE GRENADINES

Willemstad

Bonaire

Curaçao

ST GEORGE'S

St Vincent & the Grenadines

COLOMBIA

GRENADA

Tourism

Tobago

Grenada

0   250   500 km

0   125   250 miles

PORT-OF-SPAIN

TRINIDAD & TOBAGO

Trinidad & Tobago

Trinidad

V E N E Z U E L A

PANAMA

Aruba
(to Netherlands)

Netherlands Antilles
(to Netherlands)

GRENADA

CARACAS

TRINIDAD & TOBAGO

VENEZUELA

GEORGETOWN

GUYANA

PARAMARIBO

Cayenne

BOGOTÁ

SURINAME

French
Guiana
(to France)

COLOMBIA

QUITO

ECUADOR

B R A Z I L

P E R U

LIMA

B O L I V I A

LA PAZ

BRASÍLIA

SUCRE

PARAGUAY

ASUNCIÓN

Islas de los
Desventurados
(to Chile)

Juan Fernandez
Islands
(to Chile)

URUGUAY

SANTIAGO

BUENOS AIRES

MONTEVIDEO

C H I L E

A R G E N T I N A

0   500   1000 km

0   250   500 miles

Falkland Islands
(to UK)

A   C   D   E

Mighty river
The enormous Amazon river flows across South America and supports a huge variety of life there. These giant lily pads thrive in a section of slow-moving water.

SOUTH AMERICA

South America is the fourth largest continent. It stretches from the Caribbean Sea in the north to the cold lands at its southern tip. In the northeast of the continent lies the tropical Amazon Basin, where it is hot and wet all year round. The mighty Amazon river and Amazon rainforest, the world's largest rainforest, are found there. Further south the climate is cooler and there are great open plains. The longest range of mountains in the world, the Andes, extends for 7,250 km along the western edge of the continent.

Most South American countries are Spanish-speaking, and most of the continent's people live in large cities on the coast.

Rugged mountains
The Torres del Paine National Park is in the far south of Chile. Its unspoilt scenery shows the lakes and mountains at their best.

Haunting music
A young Peruvian girl plays a traditional tune on the rondador or pan-pipes. The notes are made by blowing across the top of hollow bamboo tubes.

Northern South America

The largest tropical rainforest in the world stretches across Northern South America, filling the Amazon Basin. This densely forested region is full of valuable resources, including cacao for chocolate, nuts, rare hardwoods, and plants that can be used to make medicines. But humans are rapidly destroying the rainforests by cutting down the trees for timber and to search for valuable minerals, and clearing the land for agriculture.

Brazil is the largest country in South America and covers almost half of the continent. Much of the world's coffee and sugar cane is grown there. Most of its people live in towns and cities near the coast. Brazil has a very young population – almost half the people are under 20 years old. Venezuela is the richest country in South America as it has huge oil reserves and other minerals. It also has the world's highest waterfall, Angel Falls.

The countries on the western side of the continent are dominated by the Andes Mountains, the longest mountain range in the world. Bolivia has two capitals – La Paz and Sucre. La Paz, the seat of government, high in the Andes, is the world's highest capital city.

Standing tall
The magnificent statue of Christ the Redeemer towers over Rio de Janeiro, Brazil's cultural capital, playground of the rich, and bustling Atlantic port.

ba (to Netherlands)
Netherlands Antilles
(to Netherlands)

CARACAS

lencia

Barquisimeto

Isla de
Margarita

Iron ore
mining

Maturín

TRINIDAD
& TOBAGO

Venezuela

Guyana

Suriname

FACTS AND FIGURES

Largest cities
Sao Paulo 19,037,000
Rio de Janeiro 11,571,000

Highest point
Huascarán 6,768 m

Highest waterfall
Angel Falls 978 m

Longest river
Amazon 6,448 km

Largest lake
Lake Titicaca 8,300 km²

Apure

Orinoco

Embalse
de Guri

VENEZUELA

Timber

Guiana Highlands

Cocoa

GEORGETOWN

GUYANA

PARAMARIBO

SURINAME French
Guiana
(to France)

Cayenne

Angel
Falls

Branco

Essequibo

Emerald
tree boa

Spider
monkey

Scarlet
macaw

*Mouths of
the Amazon*

Equator

IA

aviare

Orinoco

Negro

A m a z o n

Japurá

Represa de
Balbina

Piranha

Amazon

Marajó

Baía de Marajó

Belém

Amazon

Baía de São Marcos

Industry

Fortaleza

Manaus

B a s i n

Amazon

oucan

Rain forest

Tapajós

Iriri

Xingu

Sloth

*Cabo de
São Roque*

Coffee

Natal

B R A Z I L

Madeira

Purus

Brazil
nuts

Logging

São Manuel

Iuruena

Sugarcane

Bananas

Recife

Cattle

Represa de
Tucuruí

Parnaíba

Tobacco

Catedral
Basílica

Madre de Dios

Beni

Mamoré

Guaporé

Cattle

*Mato Grosso
Do Sul*

Tocantins

Araguaia

Represa de
Sobradinho

Cocoa

Salvador

B O L I V I A

Nevada
Illampu
21,061 ft.

Paper
making

Mortes

São Francisco

Soccer

Brazilian

BRASÍLIA

Mining

LA PAZ

ca

Armadillo

Goiânia

Highlands

Brazil

Oruro

SUCRE

Lake
Poopó

Tin
mining

Pantanal

Paranaíba

Coffee

Belo Horizonte

Citrus fruits

Industry

Christ the
Redeemer

evado
ajama
91 ft.

Altiplano

Corn

Paraná

Rio Grande

São Paulo

Steel making

Rio de Janeiro

CHILE

PARAGUAY

Bananas

Curitiba

A T L A N T I C

O C E A N

A R G E N T I N A

Serra Geral

Uruguay

Soy

Porto Alegre

Lagoa
dos Patos

Lagoa Mirim

0	500	1000 km
0	250	500 miles

Southern South America

Four countries make up Southern South America. They are Chile, Argentina, Paraguay and Uruguay. The Falkland Islands in the Atlantic Ocean are British territories. Chile is a long, thin country sandwiched between the ocean and the high Andes mountains. The driest place in the world, the Atacama desert, is in Chile.

Argentina has a varied landscape, including the jagged peaks of the Andes and the vast flat grasslands of the Pampas region. In the south of the country is Patagonia, a bleak plateau. At the very tip of Southern South America lies the remote and bitterly cold island of Tierra del Fuego, just 1,000 km away from Antarctica.

Uruguay and Argentina share the estuary to the Rio de la Plata, which is a great trading route to the middle of the continent. Paraguay is a landlocked country, which means it has no coasts. Most of the people there are of mixed native American and Spanish descent. In the other countries, many of the people are descendants from European settlers who arrived about 400 years ago.

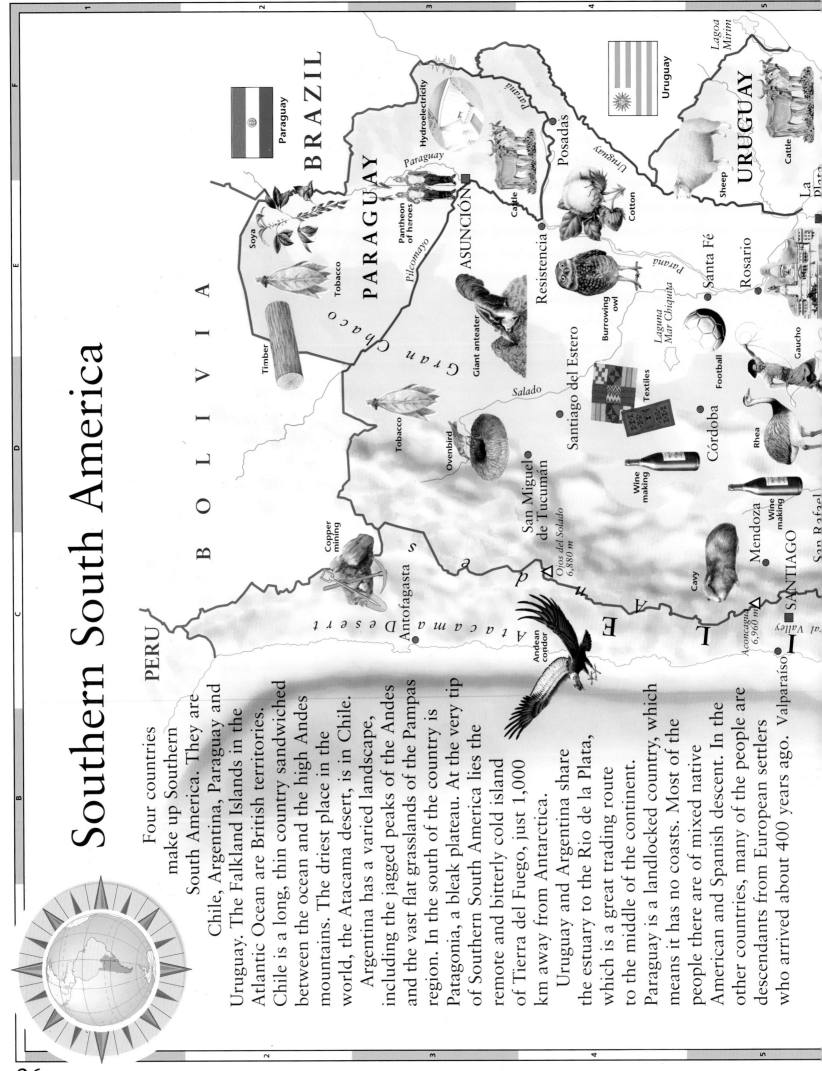

BRAZIL

Paraguay

Paraguay

Soya

Timber

Tobacco

PARAGUAY

Pantheon
of heroes

ASUNCIÓN

Pilcomayo

Hydroelectricity

Paraná

Posadas

Uruguay

Cattle

Resistencia

Cotton

Paraná

Uruguay

URUGUAY

Cattle

Sheep

La
Plata

BOLIVIA

PERU

Copper
mining

Antofagasta

Atacama Desert

Andean
condor

Gran Chaco

Giant anteater

Tobacco

Ovenbird

Salado

Santiago del Estero

Burrowing
owl

Textiles

Laguna
Mar Chiquita

Football

Córdoba

Rhea

Gaucho

San Miguel
de Tucumán

Ojos del Solado
6,880 m

Wine
making

Cavy

Mendoza

Wine
making

P a m p a s

SANTIAGO

Aconcagua
6,960 m

al Valley

Valparaíso

San Rafael

C H I L E

Santa Fé

Rosario

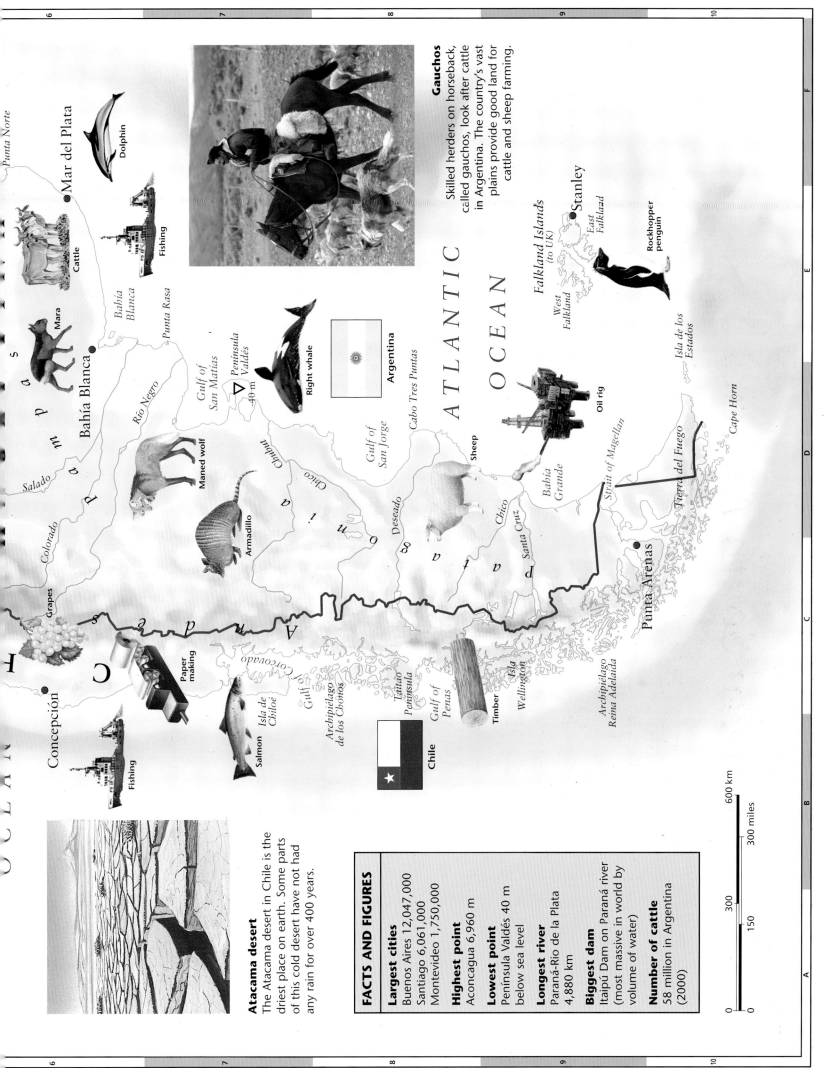

Punta Norte

Mar del Plata

Dolphin

Cattle

Fishing

Mara

Bahía Blanca

Bahía Blanca

Punta Rasa

Río Negro

Salado

P
a
m
p
a
s

Colorado

Grapes

H

Concepción

C

Fishing

Salmon

Paper making

Isla de Chiloé

Corcovado

Gulf of Corcovado

Archipiélago de los Chonos

Taitao Península

Gulf of Penas

Timber

Isla Wellington

Chile

Maned wolf

Chubut

Armadillo

Chico

P
a
t
a
g
o
n
i
a

Deseado

Gulf of San Matías

Península Valdés
40 m

Right whale

Argentina

Gulf of San Jorge

Cabo Tres Puntas

Sheep

Santa Cruz

Chico

Bahía Grande

Oil rig

Punta Arenas

Archipiélago Reina Adelaida

Strait of Magellan

Tierra del Fuego

Cape Horn

Isla de los Estados

A T L A N T I C

O C E A N

Falkland Islands (to UK)

Stanley

West Falkland

East Falkland

Rockhopper penguin

Gauchos
Skilled herders on horseback, called gauchos, look after cattle in Argentina. The country's vast plains provide good land for cattle and sheep farming.

Atacama desert
The Atacama desert in Chile is the driest place on earth. Some parts of this cold desert have not had any rain for over 400 years.

FACTS AND FIGURES

Largest cities
Buenos Aires 12,047,000
Santiago 6,061,000
Montevideo 1,750,000

Highest point
Aconcagua 6,960 m

Lowest point
Península Valdés 40 m
below sea level

Longest river
Paraná-Rio de la Plata
4,880 km

Biggest dam
Itaipú Dam on Paraná river
(most massive in world by
volume of water)

Number of cattle
58 million in Argentina
(2000)

0   150   300   600 km
0   300 miles   300 miles

Greenland
(to Denmark)

0   500   1000 km
0   250   500 miles

Jan Mayen
(to Norway)

Bjørnøya
(to Norway)

REYKJAVIK ■ ICELAND

Vesterålen
Lofoten

N O R W A Y

S W E D E N

FINLAND

R U S
F E D E

Faeroe Islands
(to Denmark)

Shetland
Islands

OSLO ■

HELSINKI ■

Outer Hebrides

Orkney
Islands

STOCKHOLM ■

TALLINN ■
ESTONIA

MOSCOW ■

UNITED
KINGDOM

Gotland
Öland

RIGA ■ LATVIA

REPUBLIC
OF IRELAND
DUBLIN ■

Isle of Man
(to UK)

DENMARK
COPENHAGEN ■

LITHUANIA
VILNIUS ■

RUSS. FED.

MINSK ■
BELARUS

NETHERLANDS
AMSTERDAM ■

LONDON ■

THE HAGUE ■

BERLIN ■

WARSAW ■

Channel Islands
(to UK)

BRUSSELS ■
BELGIUM

GERMANY

POLAND

KIEV ■

LUXEMBOURG ■
PARIS ■ LUX.

PRAGUE ■
CZECH
REPUBLIC

SLOVAKIA
BRATISLAVA ■

UKRAINE

FRANCE

VIENNA ■

BUDAPEST ■

MOLDOVA
CHIŞINĂU ■

BERN ■
SWITZ

VADUZ ■
LIECH.

AUSTRIA

HUNGARY

PORTUGAL

ANDORRA
LA VELLA ■ ANDORRA

MONACO ■

SLOVENIA
LJUBLJANA ■
ZAGREB ■
CROATIA

ROMANIA

LISBON ■

MADRID ■

SAN
MARINO

BOSNIA &
HERZEGOVINA
SARAJEVO ■

BELGRADE ■

BUCHAREST ■

SPAIN

Corsica

ITALY

SERBIA

BULGARIA

Mallorca
(Majorca)

Menorca
(Minorca)

ROME ■
VATICAN
CITY

MONTENEGRO

PODGORICA ■

SKOPJE ■
MACEDONIA

SOFIA ■

Gibraltar
(to UK)

Ibiza

Balearic Islands

Sardinia

TIRANA ■

ALBANIA

T U R K E Y

AFRICA

Sicily

MALTA ■

VALLETTA ■

GREECE

ATHENS ■

Rhodes

Crete

28

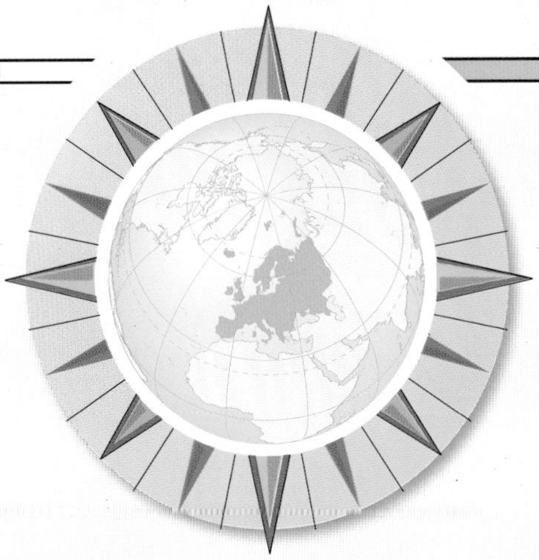

ASIA

AN

TION

EUROPE

Europe is the second smallest continent, but its 44 countries are heavily populated, making it the most crowded continent of all. It stretches from the lands fringing the Atlantic Ocean in the west to the Ural Mountains in the Russian Federation in the east, and from the Baltic Sea in the north to the Mediterranean Sea in the south. It is a continent of peninsulas and islands and its ragged coastline measures almost 61,000 km. If stretched out, this would circle the Equator just over one-and-a-half times. Much of Europe is mountainous. The countries around the Mediterranean enjoy hot, dry summers and warm, wet winters. The climate in much of the rest of Europe is quite mild.

Many of the countries in Europe have existed for hundreds of years; others have been formed very recently and are just a few years old.

National traditions
Many countries have strong traditions. These girls are dressed in the national costume of Latvia.

Rugged coastline
The Balearic Islands, shown here, are just some of the many islands and coastal regions throughout Europe that are enjoyed by visitors every year.

ASIA

Northwestern Europe

Four countries in northwestern Europe make up the area called Scandinavia: Norway, Sweden, Finland and Denmark. Far to the west of these lies the volcanic island of Iceland. The far north of Scandinavia is deep inside the Arctic Circle, but its cold climate is tempered by the North Atlantic Drift, an ocean current that carries warm water across the Atlantic Ocean.

The Scandinavian landscape is rugged, mountainous and wooded. Along the coast of Norway are long, deep sea inlets called fjords. There are also thousands of lakes – Sweden alone has over 95,000. Norway has five of the world's highest waterfalls – Utigard, Mongefossen, Espelandsfoss, Ostre Mardola Foss and Tyssestrengane. Over half of Sweden's land surface is covered with dense forest. Denmark's land, by contrast, is mainly flat, and much of it is used for farmland.

Iceland is partly covered by ice fields and glaciers. The land is volcanic and has many geysers and hot springs.

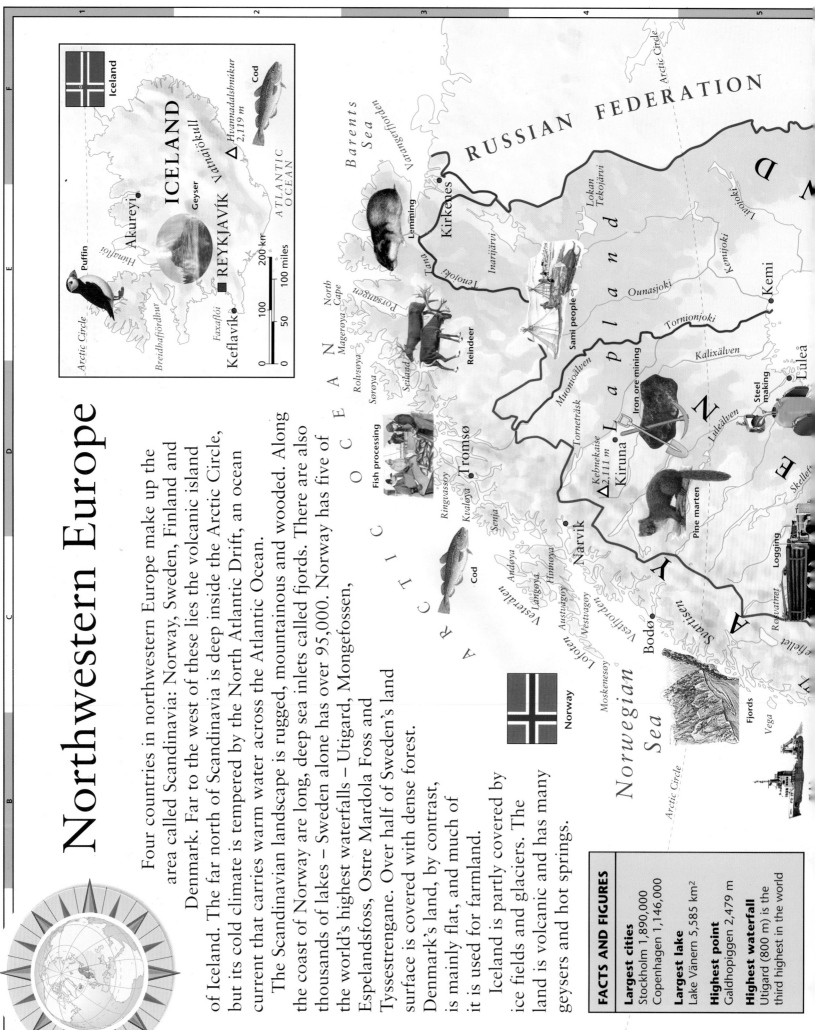

ICELAND

Iceland

REYKJAVÍK

Akureyi

Puffin

Húnaflói

Breidhafjördhur

Faxaflói

Keflavík

Arctic Circle

Geyser

Vatnajökull

△ Hvannadalshnukur 2,119 m

Cod

ATLANTIC OCEAN

200 km

100 miles

RUSSIAN FEDERATION

Barents Sea

Varangerfjorden

Lemming

Kirkenes

Tana

Teno joki

Porsangen

Magerøya

North Cape

Sørøya

Seiland

Reindeer

Rolvsøya

Fish processing

Ringvassøy

Kvaløya

Tromsø

Senja

Andøya

Langøya

Vesterålen

Hinnøya

Austvågøy

Vestvågøy

Moskenesøy

Lofoten

Norwegian Sea

Narvik

Bodø

Fjords

Vega

Arctic Circle

Norway

Inarijärvi

Lapland

Sami people

Ounasjoki

Tornionjoki

Kalixälven

Lokan Tekojärvi

Luiro

Livojoki

Kemijoki

Kemi

Luleå

Steel making

Lule älven

Iron ore mining

Kiruna

Kebnekaise △ 2,111 m

Torneträsk

Muonioälven

Pine marten

Logging

Skellefte

fjället

Rostvatnet

Svartisen

Ostre

Cod

Finland

Osprey

Timber

Mining

Kuopio

Mikkeli

Orivesi

Pielinen

Saimaa

Päijänve

Keitele

Textiles

Tampere

Industry

Vantaa

Espoo

HELSINKI

Crossbill

Long-eared bat

Vaasa (Vasa)

Turku (Åbo)

Gulf of Finland

Åland

Skiftet Kihti

Ålands hav

Fishing

Umeå

Gulf of Bothnia

Ångermanälven

Red deer

Sundsvall

Ljusnan

Storsjön

Östersund

Paper making

Pine forest

Gävle

Uppsala

STOCKHOLM

Herring

Sweden

Capercaillie

Dalälven

Iron ore mining

Mälaren

Västerås

Electronics

Norrköping

Örebro

Industry

Linköping

Industry

Jönköping

Gotland

Öland

Klarälven

Vänern

Vättern

Saab cars

Polecat

Kalmar

Denmark

Gothenburg

Industry

Helsingborg

Bornholm

Malmö

B a l t i c   S e a

Glomma

Glittertind 2,452 m

Galdhøpiggen 2,479 m

Lågen

Mjøsa

OSLO

Industry

Industry

Trondheim

Industry

Skiing

Waterfalls

Dovrefjell

Jotunheimen

Lillehammer

Hydroelectricity

Hardangervidda

Cattle

Arendal

Kristiansand

Herring

Skagerrak

Kattegat

Ålborg

Århus

Pigs

Jutland

D E N M A R K

COPENHAGEN

Zealand

Industry

Falster

Store Bælt

Fyn

Lolland

Odense

Esbjerg

Lego

Oil rig

Ålesund

Smøla

Averøya

Hitra

Frøya

Trondheimsfjorden

Jostedalsbreen

Stave church

Sognefjorden

Bergen

Industry

Boknafjorden

Stavanger

Mining

Setesdal

North Sea

Fishing

Famous fjords

Norway's coastline is famous for its deep sea inlets, called fjords. During the last Ice Age, glaciers gouged great hollows in the land. When the ice melted and the sea level rose, these troughs filled with water.

400 km

200 miles

200

100

0

0

The British Isles

The British Isles are made up of two large islands and many smaller ones that lie off the coast of northwest Europe, surrounded by the Atlantic Ocean. The two larger islands are Great Britain and Ireland. Great Britain consists of England, Scotland and Wales, which together with the northern part of Ireland, called Northern Ireland, make up the United Kingdom. The rest of Ireland, the Republic of Ireland, is a separate country.

The British Isles enjoy a mild climate, which is influenced by the warm Gulf Stream. This is an ocean current that carries warm water from the Straits of Florida across the Atlantic towards western Europe, helping to keep the area warm. Winters can be snowy and wet, with cold winds coming from the north or east. Summers are generally warm, although winds from the southwest do bring rain.

Much of the land is used for farming. But nearly 90 per cent of the population live in towns and cities. In the 19th century CE, many factories were built and big cities grew to support them. Today, the factories have declined, and more people work in service industries, such as banking and insurance.

London's skyline
The dome of St Paul's Cathedral stands high above the surrounding buildings. Built by Sir Christopher Wren in CE1672, the dome is one of the finest in the world.

Shetland Islands
Mainland
Lerwick
Fair Isle

Fishing

Orkney Islands
Mainland
Kirkwall
Hoy

Grey seal

Seagull

Cod

Wick

Sheep

Oil rig

Aberdeen

Don
Dee
Spey
Red deer
Ben Macdhui 1,309 m
SCOTLAND
Dundee
Perth
Edinburgh castle
Firth of Forth

Inverness
Loch Ness
Grampian Mountains
skiing
Ben Nevis 1,343 m
Fort William
Oban
Mull
Colonsay

Cape Wrath

Puffin

The Minch

Skye
Rhum
Eigg
Muck
Canna
Coll
Tiree
Barra

Lewis
Harris
North Uist
South Uist

Saint Kilda

Outer Hebrides

The Little Minch

Inner Hebrides

Northwest Highlands

Moray Firth

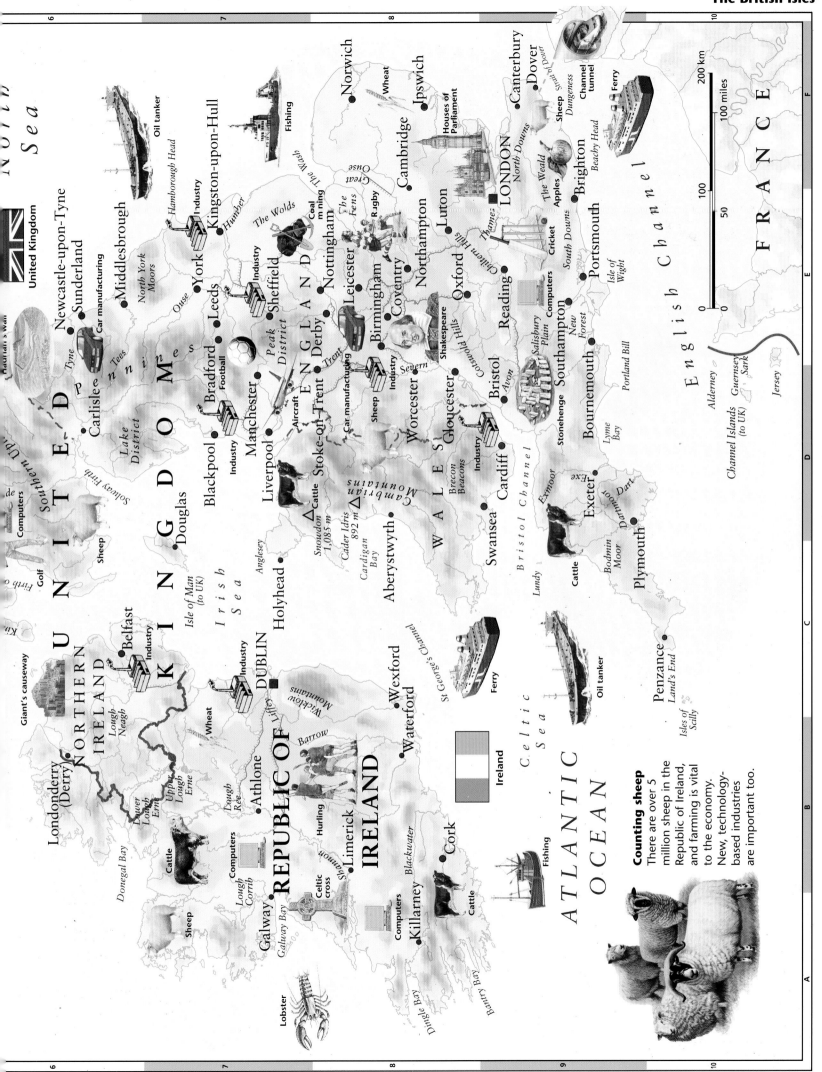

Counting sheep
There are over 5 million sheep in the Republic of Ireland, and farming is vital to the economy. New, technology-based industries are important too.

Germany and the Low Countries

Belgium, the Netherlands and Luxembourg are small countries where the land is low and flat. Because of this, they are also known as the Low Countries. About 40 per cent of the land in the Netherlands has been reclaimed from the sea. To hold back the water, dykes or sea walls have been built. The reclaimed land is excellent farming land and the Netherlands is known for its agricultural goods, especially dairy products and flowers. Belgium, too, is mostly flat, and also relies on dykes to hold back the sea. Much of tiny Luxembourg is rolling plateau land, and fertile farmland is found here.

Germany is a large country – the fourth largest in Europe. The central area is made up of highlands and plateaux. The Bohemian Forest is found further south. Further south still are the Bavarian Alps, which border Austria. The Black Forest, in the southwest of the country, is mountainous and popular with tourists.

All four countries are prosperous and their people enjoy a high standard of living. Belgium's capital, Brussels, contains the major offices of the European Union. Luxembourg is an important banking centre. Germany was divided into two countries, East Germany and West Germany, for 45 years before it became one country again in 1990. It is now Europe's leading industrial country.

Living in the cold

The climate in the higher areas of the Black Forest, in Germany, is raw and cold in winter, but the valleys are mild and have good pasture lands. Winter sports are popular here. The distinctive houses are built with steeply sloping roofs so that any snow will slide off them.

FACTS AND FIGURES

Largest cities
Berlin 4,201,000
Stuttgart 2,626,000
Hamburg 2,549,000

Highest mountain
Zugspitze 2,963 m

Longest river
Danube 2,858 km

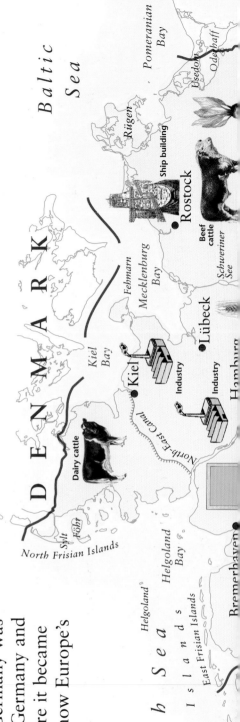

Baltic Sea

Pomeranian Bay

Usedom

Oderhaff

Rügen

Ship building

Rostock

Beef cattle

Schweriner See

Mecklenburg Bay

Lübeck

Febmarn Bay

Kiel Bay

D E N M A R K

Kiel

Industry

Industry

Hamburg

North-East Canal

Dairy cattle

Sylt

Föhr

North Frisian Islands

N o r t h   S e a

Helgoland

Helgoland Bay

East Frisian Islands

F r i s i a n   I s l a n d s

Frisian Islands

Bremerhaven

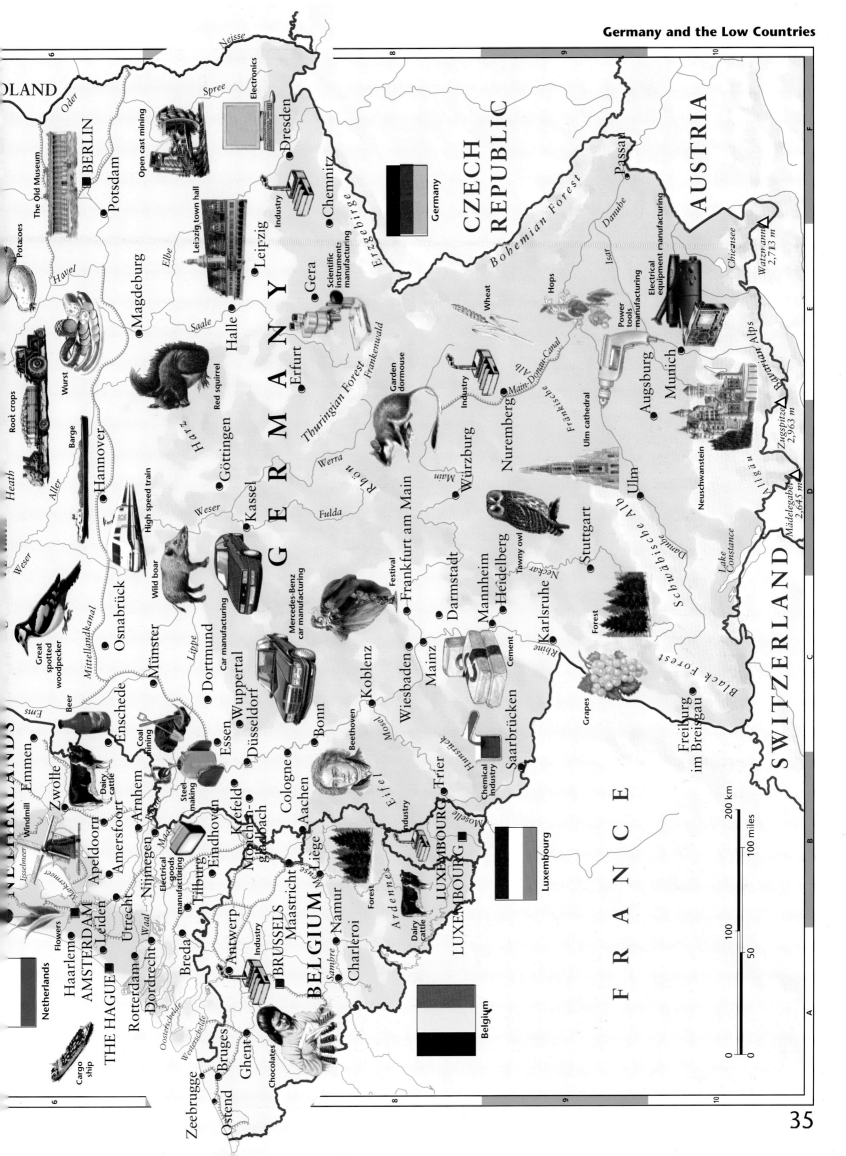

POLAND

Oder

Neisse

Spree

BERLIN

The Old Museum

Potatoes

Havel

Heath

Potsdam

Open cast mining

Electronics

Dresden

Industry

Chemnitz

Leipzig town hall

Magdeburg

Leipzig

Gera

Scientific instruments manufacturing

Erzgebirge

CZECH REPUBLIC

Germany

Bohemian Forest

Passau

AUSTRIA

Danube

Isar

Chiemsee

Watzmann 2,713 m

Hops

Electrical equipment manufacturing

Wheat

Power tools manufacturing

Augsburg

Munich

Bavarian Alps

Zugspitze 2,963 m

Mädelegabel 2,645 m

Allgäu

Saale

Halle

Elbe

Erfurt

Red squirrel

Göttingen

Harz

Thuringian Forest

Frankenwald

Rhön

Garden dormouse

Industry

Würzburg

Main

Main-Donau-Canal

Nuremberg

Fränkische Alb

Ulm cathedral

Ulm

Neuschwanstein

Schwäbische Alb

Lake Constance

Root crops

Wurst

Barge

Hannover

Aller

Weser

Weser

Kassel

Werra

Fulda

Frankfurt am Main

Festival

Darmstadt

Mannheim

Heidelberg

Tawny owl

Neckar

Stuttgart

Karlsruhe

Schwäbische Alb

Danube

NETHERLANDS

Ems

Great spotted woodpecker

High speed train

Wild boar

Mercedes-Benz car manufacturing

Mittellandkanal

Osnabrück

Münster

Lippe

Dortmund

Car manufacturing

Essen

Wuppertal

Düsseldorf

Bonn

Beethoven

Koblenz

Mosel

Wiesbaden

Mainz

Rhine

Cement

Saarbrücken

Chemical industry

Trier

Grapes

Freiburg im Breisgau

Black Forest

Forest

SWITZERLAND

Beer

Dairy cattle

Coal mining

Steel making

Enschede

Arnhem

Rhine

Krefeld

Mönchen-gladbach

Cologne

Aachen

Eifel

Hunsrück

Moselle

LUXEMBOURG

LUXEMBOURG

Luxembourg

Windmill

IJsselmeer

Zwolle

Emmen

Apeldoorn

Amersfoort

Utrecht

Nijmegen

Waal

Maas

Electrical goods manufacturing

Eindhoven

Tilburg

Breda

Mosa

Ardennes

Forest

Dairy cattle

FRANCE

Markermeer

Flowers

Haarlem

AMSTERDAM

Leiden

THE HAGUE

Rotterdam

Dordrecht

Oosterschelde

Westerschelde

Breda

Antwerp

Industry

BRUSSELS

Maastricht

Liège

BELGIUM

Namur

Charleroi

Sambre

Meuse

Netherlands

Cargo ship

Zeebrugge

Ostend

Bruges

Ghent

Chocolates

Belgium

200 km

100 miles

100

50

35

G E R M A N Y

France

France is the largest country in western Europe. The land changes greatly across the country. In the northeast the Vosges Mountains form a border with Germany, while the Alps separate France from Italy. The southwestern border is formed by the Pyrenees, and to the west is the Atlantic Ocean. There are rugged highlands in central France, and also many beautiful river valleys. Corsica, the fourth largest island in the Mediterranean, belongs to France.

The climate varies across such a large area, which means that many different crops can be grown. These include wheat, maize, peaches and grapes, which are made into some of the world's finest wines. French food is also of high quality and French cooking is enjoyed all over the world.

Tourism plays a large part in the French economy. Every year, thousands of people enjoy holidays along the warm Mediterranean coast, in the French countryside or in the cold, snowy mountainous regions, where winter sports such as skiing are popular.

The tiny nation of Monaco, on the south coast near the Italian border, is the second smallest independent country in the world.

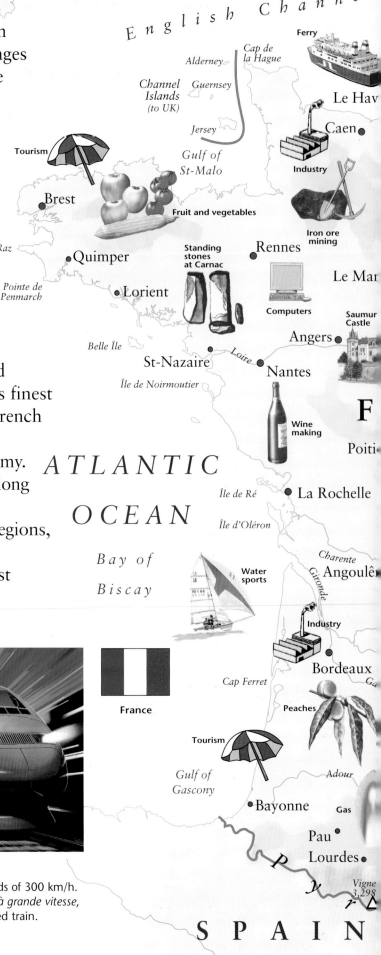

FACTS AND FIGURES

Largest cities
Paris 9,645,000
Marseille 1,350,000
Lyon 1,349,000

Longest river
Loire 1,020 km

Highest mountain
Mont Blanc 4,810 m. This is the highest mountain in Alpine Europe

Number of tourists
75 million visitors per year (2000)

High-speed travel
TGVs can travel at speeds of 300 km/h. TGV stands for *le train à grande vitesse*, which means high speed train.

Fine wines
Vineyards of grapes grow throughout much of France, to be made into wines and spirits.

Spain and Portugal

The countries of Spain, Portugal and tiny Andorra make up the Iberian Peninsula, a land mass that juts out from southern Europe. It has a varied landscape, with mountains called sierras and a broad central plateau. The lands along the northern and western coasts are fertile farming regions and benefit from Atlantic rains. Madrid, in the heart of Spain, bakes under the hot summer sun, but has cold winters. It is the capital of Spain, and is a lively and bustling city, where the people love to party.

Further south on the Mediterranean coast, the climate is hotter, making the region popular with tourists. The climate along the coasts of Portugal is cooler, with warm summers and milder winters.

Andorra is a tiny country high in the Pyrenees. Winters there can be harsh, with lots of snow, but summers are sunny and dry.

Gibraltar is a tiny British colony, linked to Spain by a narrow strip of land only 3 km long.

FACTS AND FIGURES

Largest cities
Madrid 6,163,000
Barcelona 4,973,000
Lisbon 2,571,000

Longest river
Tagus 1,007 km

Highest mountain
Mulhacén 3,478 m

Highest capital
Andorra La Vella is the highest capital city in Europe

Bay of Biscay

A Coruña

Santiago de Compostela

Gijón

Oviedo

Co

Brown bear

Cordillera Cantábric

León

Vigo

Miño

Ourense

Mining

Whe

Wine making

Potatoes

Mining

Embalse de Ricobayo

Valladol

Porto

Douro

Embalse de Almendra

Salamanca

Grapes

Potatoes

Coimbra

Serra da Estrela

S

PORTUGAL

S

I

Portugal

Embalse de Alcántara

Tagus

Embalse de Valdec

Santarém

Cáceres

Embalse de Cijara

Tagus

Industry

LISBON

Cork trees

Badajoz

Sheep

Setúbal

Alqueva Reservoir

Cabo Espichel

Alentejo

Guadiana

Sierra Morena

Great M at Cor

Córdo

Sardines

Iberian lynx

Guadalquivir

Seville

Flamenco dancers

Tourism

Algarve

Citrus fruit

Huelva

Dos Hermanas

Tavira

Wine making

Lagos

Faro

Gulf of Cádiz

Jerez de la Frontera

Barbary ape

Cabo de São Vicente

Fishing

Costa de la Luz

Cádiz

Si

Marbel

ATLANTIC OCEAN

Tuna

Gibralta (to UK)

Strait of Gibraltar

Ceuta (to Sp

Fishing

F · G · H · I · J

0 — 100 — 200 km
0 — 50 — 100 miles

Gulf of Gascony

Fishing

de Santander

Bilbao   Donostia-
San Sebastián

F R A N C E

Pyrenees

Skiing

Andorra

Gulf of Lion

Vitoria-Gasteiz   Pamplona

Burgos

Sheep

Aneto 3,404 m △
ANDORRA LA VELLA

■ ANDORRA
Llívia (to Spain)

Segre

Wild boar

Textiles

Chamois

Ibex

Ebro

Zaragoza

Grapes

Olives

Car
manufacturing

Girona

Costa Brava

Duero

Real de
anzanares

*Embalse
de Mequinenza*

Tarragona

Barcelona

Sagrada Familia

Bullfighting

■ MADRID

A   I   N

edo ●A

Sistema Ibérico

a Central

Castelló
de la Plana

Costa del Azahar

Tourism

Balearic Islands

Menorca
(Minorca)

Palma de Mallorca

Mallorca
(Majorca)

Tourism

Grapes

Almonds

Citrus
fruit

Valencia

*Gulf of
Valencia*

Tourism

Ibiza

Fishing

Júcar

Albacete

*Cabo de
la Nao*

Formentera

Guadiana

Segura

Tourism

Alicante

Elche
(Elx)

Costa Blanca

M e d i t e r r a n e a n
S e a

Linares

Murcia

Alhambra
Palace

Cabo de Palos

Cartagena

as Béticos

Granada *Nevada*

Sierra △ *Mulhacén
3,478 m*

Almería

Sailing

Spain

ála ga

Tourism

*Cabo
de Gata*

sta del Sol

Fishing

Going fishing
Portugal has a long Atlantic coastline and
many Portuguese make a living from fishing.
Sardines, cod, hake and halibut are all caught.

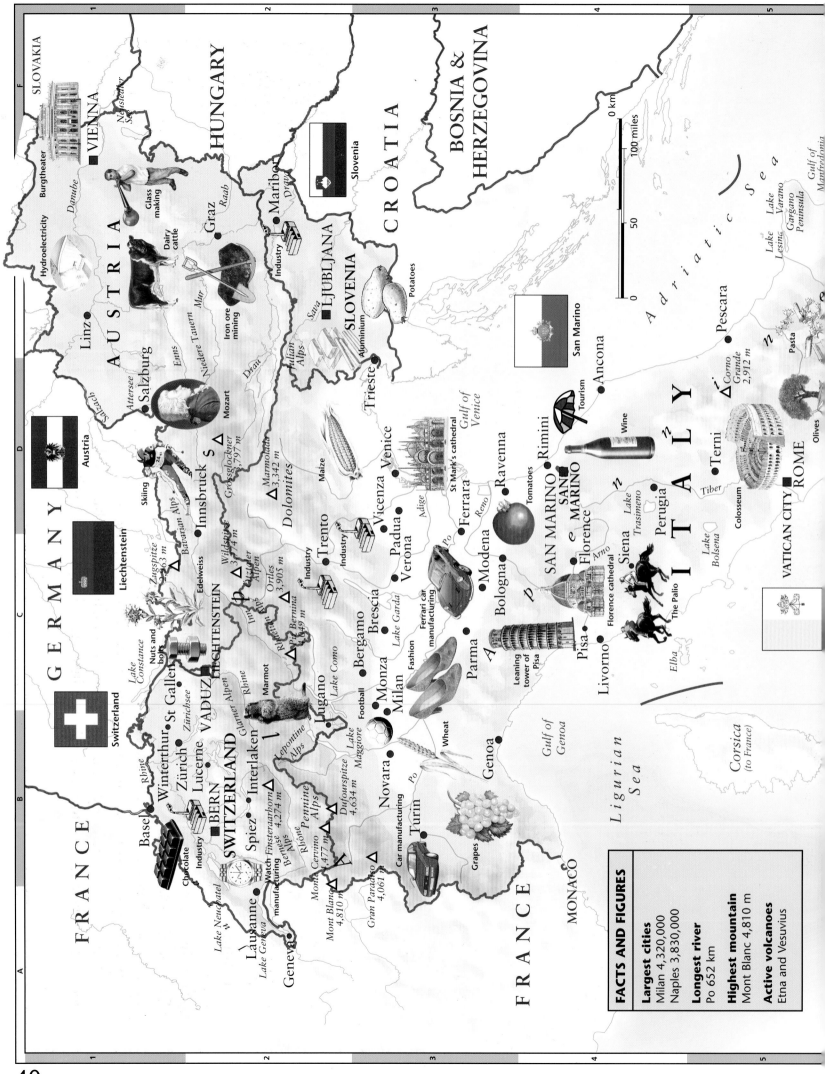

SLOVAKIA

VIENNA

Burgtheater

Neusiedler See

Hydroelectricity

Danube

Glass making

HUNGARY

Dairy cattle

Graz

Raab

Maribor

Drava

Industry

LJUBLJANA

SLOVENIA

Slovenia

CROATIA

BOSNIA & HERZEGOVINA

Linz

AUSTRIA

Salzburg

Attersee

Mozart

Iron ore mining

Mur

Niedere Tauern

Enns

Julian Alps

Sava

Potatoes

Aluminium

Salzach

Trieste

San Marino

Ancona

Pescara

Adriatic Sea

Gulf of Manfredonia

Lake Varano

Lake Lesina

Gargano Peninsula

Austria

GERMANY

Skiing

Innsbruck

Grossglockner 3,797 m

Marmolada 3,342 m

Dolomites

Maize

Vicenza

Venice

Gulf of Venice

St Mark's cathedral

Ferrara

Reno

Ravenna

Tomatoes

Rimini

SAN MARINO

SAN MARINO

Wine

ITALY

Terni

Corno Grande 2,912 m

Pasta

Olives

ROME

Liechtenstein

Zugspitze 2,963 m

Bavarian Alps

Edelweiss

Wildspitze 3,774 m

Ötztaler Alpen

Ortles 3,905 m

Inn

Trento

Industry

Adige

Po

Padua

Verona

Modena

Bologna

Po

Florence

Arno

Florence cathedral

Perugia

Lake Trasimeno

Siena

The Palio

Lake Bolsena

Tiber

Colosseum

VATICAN CITY

Lake Constance

Nuts and bolts

LIECHTENSTEIN

VADUZ

Rhine

Marmot

Glarner Alpen

Piz Bernina 4,049 m

Rätikon

Industry

Bergamo

Brescia

Lake Garda

Ferrari car manufacturing

Parma

Leaning tower of Pisa

Pisa

Pistoia

Elba

SWITZERLAND

Zürichsee

St Gallen

Winterthur

Zürich

Lucerne

BERN

Interlaken

Spiez

Lugano

Lake Como

Football

Monza

Milan

Fashion

Livorno

Ligurian Sea

Corsica (to France)

Lake Neuchâtel

Basel

Rhine

Chocolate

Industry

Watch manufacturing

Finsteraarhorn 4,274 m

Bernese Alps

Rhône

Pennine Alps

Monte Cervino 4,477 m

Lepontine Alps

Lake Maggiore

Novara

Wheat

Po

Genoa

Gulf of Genoa

Lausanne

Geneva

Lake Geneva

Mont Blanc 4,810 m

Gran Paradiso 4,061 m

Dufourspitze 4,634 m

Turin

Car manufacturing

Grapes

FRANCE

MONACO

FRANCE

FRANCE

FACTS AND FIGURES

Largest cities
Milan 4,320,000
Naples 3,830,000

Longest river
Po 652 km

Highest mountain
Mont Blanc 4,810 m

Active volcanoes
Etna and Vesuvius

0 km

100 miles

50

0

The Alpine States and Italy

The Alpine States – Switzerland, Austria and Slovenia – take their name from the mountain ranges known as the Alps. These jagged peaks have year-round snow. Winter sports are important there, and in many places, cable cars carry tourists and skiers high into the snow fields.

The Alps form the northern border of Italy and overlook the most fertile and densely populated part of the country – the northern plains. Another range of mountains, the Apenines, forms a backbone down the middle of the country. Italy also has a chain of volcanoes, stretching from Vesuvius, near Naples, to Etna on the island of Sicily. Both Sicily and Sardinia belong to Italy. Further south still are the islands that make up the Republic of Malta.

Two independent countries are found inside Italy. They are San Marino, which lies east of the Apenines, and the Vatican City State, which is the world's smallest independent nation and lies inside Italy's own capital, Rome.

High mountains
The Dolomites are mountains that lie to the north of Italy and form part of the Alps. Snow covers these peaks all year and they are home to many glaciers.

Capo Santa Maria di Leuca

Grapes

Taranto

Gulf of Taranto

Capo Colonna

Porcupine

Basento

Olives

Gulf of Squillace

Reggio di Calabria

Capo Spartivento

Appennino Lucano

Messina

Strait of Messina

Ionian Sea

Citrus fruit

Stromboli volcano

Stromboli

Catania

Siracusa

Mount Etna 3,350 m

Vesuvius 1,279 m

Naples

Salerno

Gulf of Salerno

Capri

Ischia

Gaeta

Aeolian Islands

Sicily

Olives

Capo Passero

Ponziane Islands

Ustica

Oranges

Palermo

Tyrrhenian Sea

Marsala

Capo San Vito

Strait of Sicily

Grapes

Pantelleria

Malta Channel

VALLETTA

MALTA

Malta

Gozo

Fishing

Malta

Linosa

Pelagic Islands

Lampedusa

Italy

Ferry

Mediterranean Sea

Sassari

Olives

Turso

Punta la Marmora 1,834 m

Sardinia

Tourism

Grapes

Cagliari

Capo Carbonara

Capo Spartivento

San Antioco

Eastern and Central Europe

Eastern and Central Europe is a region of cold winters and warm summers. In some places, such as in Latvia, winter temperatures drop so low that the seas freeze over. Further inland, too, bitterly cold winters are usual.

During the 1980s and 1990s, many of the countries in this area underwent huge political changes. Czechoslovakia split into two separate countries – the Czech Republic and Slovakia. Nations that had previously belonged to the Soviet Union also broke away to become independent countries. These are the Baltic states (Estonia, Latvia and Lithuania), Belarus, the Ukraine and Moldova.

Poland shares its borders with seven other countries, but still has a coastline. Gdansk in the north is a major ship-building area. The Czech Republic is a hilly, landlocked country in the middle of Europe.

The Ukraine is the second largest country in Europe. Great quantities of wheat are grown there – it was once known as the 'breadbasket of the Soviet Union'. Hungary has plains and rolling hills. Estonia is a land of flat plains and lakes. It also has more than 800 islands.

FACTS AND FIGURES

Largest cities
Kiev 2,810,000
Warsaw 2,250,000
Budapest 1,881,000

Longest river
Danube 2,858 km

Highest mountain
Gerlachovsky Stit 2,666 m

TALLINN

ESTONIA

Pigs

Tartu

Dairy cattle

Lake Peipus

Lake Pskov

Estonia

RIGA

Potatoes

LATVIA

Latvia

Lithuania

Daugavpils

Beef cattle

Western Dvina

Churches in Vilnius

Beautiful city
Prague, the capital of the Czech Republic, has been a bustling city for over 500 years. It has been a centre of culture, learning and the arts and is a popular tourist destination.

ANIA

Chemical industry

unas

VILNIUS

Flax

Vitsyebsk

P   l   a   i   n

Machinery

Sugar beet

MINSK

Berezina

Vegetables

Barley

Eggs

Poultry

0   200   400 km

0   100   200 miles

BELARUS

Pripet

Pigs

Dnieper

Homyel

Belarus

RUSSIAN

FEDERATION

Brest

Pripet Marshes

Dnieper Lowlands

Common hamster

Ukraine

Wheat farming

Chernobyl

Kiev Reservoir

Industry

KIEV

Desna

Steppe polecat

Kharkiv

Donets

Titanium mining

Saint Sophia cathedral

UKRAINE

Volyn-Podolian Upland

Kremenchuk Reservoir

Steel making

Industry

Lviv

Oil

Wheat farming

Coal mining

Maize

Dnipropetrovsk

Donetsk

Chernivtsi

Dniester

Sunflowers

Southern Bug

Cossack dancers

Kakhovka Reservoir

Maize

Mariupol

Gulf of Taganrog

MOLDOVA

Black Sea Lowland

Sunflowers

Hungary

Moldova

CHISINAU

Grapes

Prut

Odesa

Gas

Sea of Azov

Kerch

ROMANIA

Sunflowers

Black Sea

Crimean Peninsula

Sevastopol

Southeastern Europe

Much of Southeastern Europe is mountainous. Farmers graze their sheep and goats on the slopes, while growing crops such as grains and grapes on the lower land. The climate is changeable – winters are usually bitterly cold, especially in the north, while the south enjoys milder winters and extremely hot, dry summers. The coastlines along the Adriatic, Black and Mediterranean seas, and especially the islands in the Aegean Sea, are all popular with tourists. Bosnia & Herzegovina has the shortest coastline in the region – just 20 km on the Adriatic coast.

War has taken its toll in this area. During the 1990s, the peoples of Yugoslavia fought bitterly and divided their country into six new countries – Bosnia & Herzegovina, Croatia, Macedonia, Montenegro, Serbia and Slovenia. Today, these countries are beginning to rebuild stable societies.

Greece is a rugged country with many islands. It is also one of the oldest civilizations in Europe. Ancient cultures thrived here, and many fantastic ruins remain to this day.

Gathering roses

Agriculture is very important in Southeastern Europe and many of its people make their living from the land. Here, two young women are hard at work harvesting roses on a farm in Bulgaria.

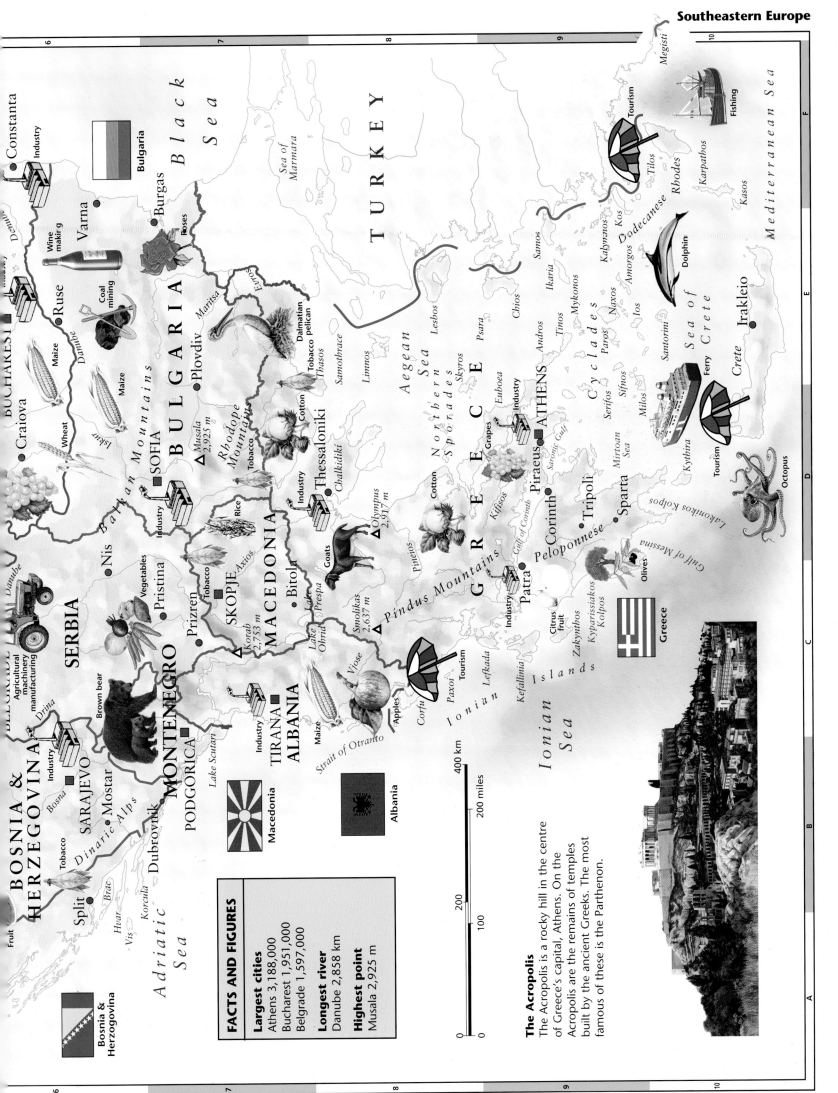

Bulgaria

Black Sea

Constanta
Industry
Varna
Burgas
Roses
Wine making
Ruse
Coal mining
Danube
Maize
Maize
Wheat
Iskur
Craiova
BUCHAREST

Sea of Marmara

T U R K E Y

Megisti
Tourism
Fishing
Tilos
Rhodes
Karpathos
Kasos
Dodecanese
Kos
Kalymnos
Amorgos
Naxos
Dolphin

Mediterranean Sea

Maritsa
Plovdiv
B U L G A R I A
SOFIA
△ Musala 2,925 m
Rhodope Mountains
Tobacco
Industry
Balkan Mountains
Cotton
Thessaloniki
Chalkidiki
Tobacco pellican
Dalmatian
Thasos
Samothrace
Limnos
Lesbos
Psara
Chios
Samos
Ikaria
Tinos
Mykonos
Andros
Euboea
Skyros
Northern Sporades
Aegean Sea
Sea of Crete
Santorini
Crete
Irakleio
Ferry
Tourism
Octopus
Kythira
Lakonikos Kolpos
Sparta
Tripoli
Corinth
Piraeus
ATHENS
Industry
Grapes
Cotton
Kifisos
Gulf of Corinth
Saronic Gulf
Mirtoan Sea
Milos
Sifnos
Serifos
Paros
Naxos
Ios
Kea
Cyclades
G R E E C E

Maritsa
Evros
Maize
Rice
SKOPJE
Axios
M A C E D O N I A
Bitola
△ Korab 2,753 m
Lake Ohrid
Lake Prespa
Goats
△ Olympus 2,917 m
Pineios
△ Smolikas 2,637 m
Pindus Mountains
Olives

Industry
Patra
Peloponnese
Citrus fruit
Kyparissiakos Kolpos
Zakynthos
Kefallinia
Lefkada
Ionian Islands
Corfu
Paxoi
Tourism
Ionian Sea

S E R B I A
Nis
Pristina
Prizren
Vegetables
Tobacco
Danube
Agricultural machinery manufacturing
Drina
Bosna
SARAJEVO
Mostar
Dubrovnik
PODGORICA
MONTENEGRO
Industry
Brown bear
Dinaric Alps
Lake Scutari
TIRANA
ALBANIA
Industry
Maize
Vjose
Strait of Otranto
Apples
Tourism

BOSNIA & HERZEGOVINA
Tobacco
Split
Brac
Hvar
Vis
Korcula
Adriatic Sea
Fruit

Macedonia

Albania

FACTS AND FIGURES

Largest cities
Athens 3,188,000
Bucharest 1,951,000
Belgrade 1,597,000

Longest river
Danube 2,858 km

Highest point
Musala 2,925 m

400 km
200 miles
200
100
0
0

Bosnia & Herzegovina

Greece

The Acropolis
The Acropolis is a rocky hill in the centre of Greece's capital, Athens. On the Acropolis are the remains of temples built by the ancient Greeks. The most famous of these is the Parthenon.

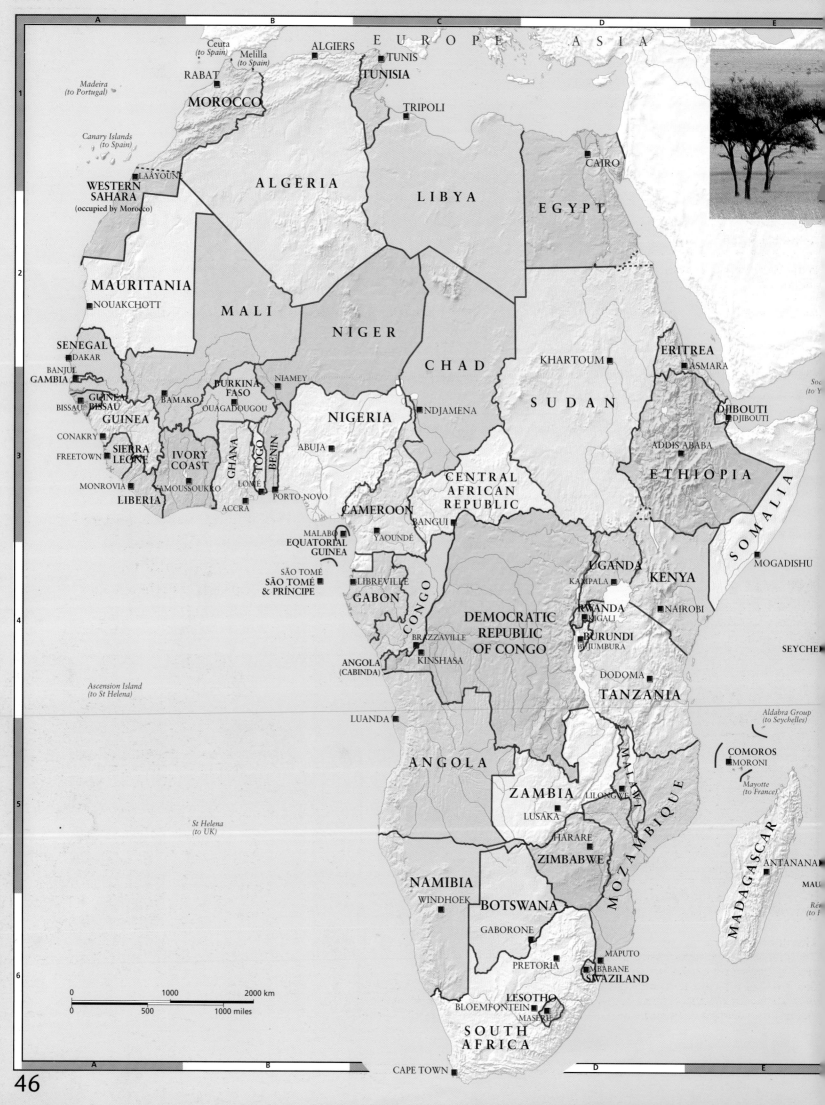

Going green
During the wet season, lush grass grows in the Masai Mara game reserve in Kenya, and the trees burst into life. Animals, including wildebeest, gazelles, giraffes and lions, come to feast on the fresh foods.

AFRICA

Africa is the second largest continent, making up about 20 per cent of the earth's land mass. It is almost completely surrounded by water. Only a narrow finger of land at Suez in Egypt connects the continent with Asia. When seen from space, Africa looks as if it can be divided into three broad bands. The northern part is mainly covered by the Sahara – the largest hot desert in the world. The middle band lies across the Equator and is covered with tropical grasslands and rainforests. The grasslands, or savannah, are home to most of Africa's large wildlife, including elephants, rhinos, lions and leopards. Further south, the lands become drier again. The Great Rift Valley, a crack in the earth's crust, runs through East Africa. Mountains, gorges and deep lakes, including Lake Victoria, mark its course. The Nile, the longest river in the world, is found in Africa.

There are over 50 separate nations in Africa. These are home to many different peoples and cultures.

Lifeblood of Egypt
The River Nile rises in eastern Africa and flows through Egypt, towards the Mediterranean Sea. It has been a major transport route for over 5,000 years. Traditional boats, such as this felucca, still travel its waters today.

Living in Africa
There are lots of children in Africa as the population is growing fast. In many places it is difficult to provide enough schools for everyone.

Northern Africa

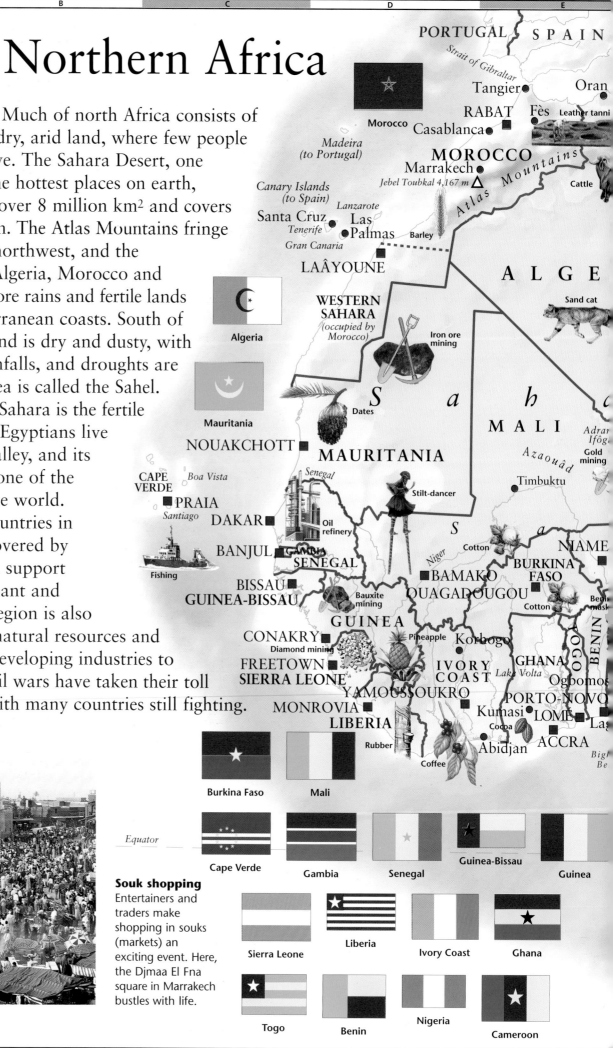

Much of north Africa consists of dry, arid land, where few people live. The Sahara Desert, one of the hottest places on earth, stretches over 8 million km² and covers much of the region. The Atlas Mountains fringe the desert in the northwest, and the countries here – Algeria, Morocco and Tunisia – enjoy more rains and fertile lands along the Mediterranean coasts. South of the Sahara, the land is dry and dusty, with unpredictable rainfalls, and droughts are common. This area is called the Sahel. To the east of the Sahara is the fertile Nile valley. Most Egyptians live within the Nile valley, and its capital, Cairo, is one of the busiest cities in the world.

Many of the countries in west Africa are covered by rainforests, which support a varied mix of plant and animal life. The region is also relatively rich in natural resources and minerals, and is developing industries to process them. Civil wars have taken their toll in recent times, with many countries still fighting.

PORTUGAL SPAIN
Strait of Gibraltar
Tangier · Oran
RABAT · Fès · Leather tanni
Morocco Casablanca
Madeira
(to Portugal)
MOROCCO
Marrakech ·
Canary Islands
(to Spain) · Lanzarote
Santa Cruz · Las
Tenerife · Palmas · Barley
Gran Canaria
LAÂYOUNE
Jebel Toubkal 4,167 m △ Atlas Mountains
Cattle
Algeria
WESTERN
SAHARA
(occupied by
Morocco)
A L G E
Sand cat
Iron ore
mining
Mauritania
Dates
S *a* **h** *a*
M A L I Adrar
Ifôg...
NOUAKCHOTT · *Azaouâd* Gold
mining
MAURITANIA
Timbuktu
CAPE *Boa Vista*
VERDE *Senegal*
· PRAIA Stilt-dancer
Santiago Oil
DAKAR · refinery **S** *a*
Niger Cotton
BANJUL · **NIAME**
BISSAU · GAMBIA BAMAKO **BURKINA**
SENEGAL OUAGADOUGOU **FASO**
GUINEA-BISSAU Bauxite Cotton Beni...
mining mask
GUINEA Cotton
CONAKRY · Pineapple Korhogo
Diamond mining **GHANA**
FREETOWN **IVORY** TOGO BENIN
SIERRA LEONE **COAST** Lake Volta Ogbomos...
YAMOUSSOUKRO PORTO-NOVO
MONROVIA · Kumasi · LOME La...
LIBERIA Cocoa
Rubber ACCRA
· Abidjan Big...
Coffee Be...

Burkina Faso | Mali

Equator

Cape Verde | Gambia | Senegal | Guinea-Bissau | Guinea

Sierra Leone | Liberia | Ivory Coast | Ghana

Souk shopping
Entertainers and traders make shopping in souks (markets) an exciting event. Here, the Djmaa El Fna square in Marrakech bustles with life.

Togo | Benin | Nigeria | Cameroon

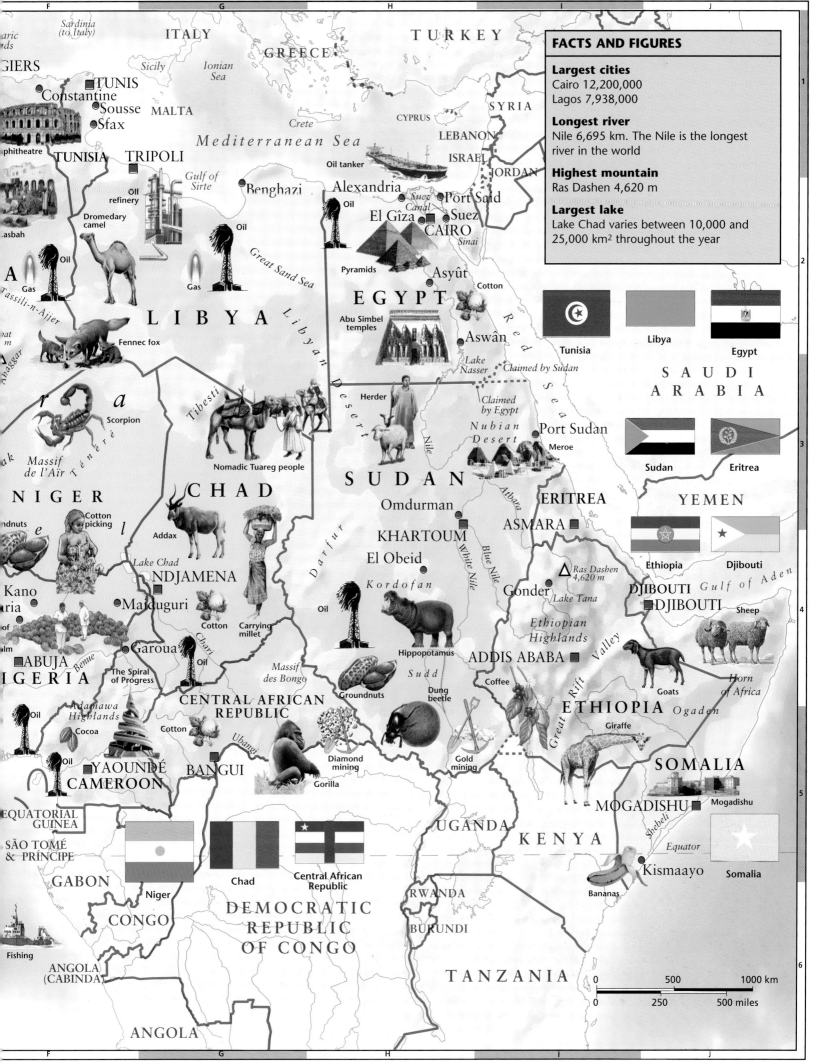

FACTS AND FIGURES

Largest cities
Cairo 12,200,000
Lagos 7,938,000

Longest river
Nile 6,695 km. The Nile is the longest
river in the world

Highest mountain
Ras Dashen 4,620 m

Largest lake
Lake Chad varies between 10,000 and
25,000 km² throughout the year

ITALY
GREECE
TURKEY
Sardinia
(to Italy)
GIERS
TUNIS
Constantine
Sousse
Sfax
Sicily
Ionian
Sea
MALTA
Crete
SYRIA
CYPRUS
LEBANON
ISRAEL
JORDAN
TUNISIA
TRIPOLI
Mediterranean Sea
Gulf of
Sirte
Benghazi
Oil tanker
Alexandria
Port Said
Suez
Canal
Suez
El Gîza
CAIRO
Sinai
Oil refinery
Dromedary
camel
Oil
Oil
Great Sand Sea
Gas
Gas
Pyramids
EGYPT
Asyût
Cotton
LIBYA
Libyan Desert
Abu Simbel
temples
Aswân
Lake
Nasser
Claimed by Sudan
Red Sea
SAUDI
ARABIA
Tassili-n-Ajjer
Oil
Gas
Fennec fox
Tibesti
Herder
Claimed
by Egypt
Nubian
Desert
Port Sudan
Meroe
r   a
Scorpion
Massif
de l'Air
Nomadic Tuareg people
SUDAN
Nile
Atbara
ERITREA
YEMEN
NIGER
Cotton
picking
Addax
CHAD
Omdurman
KHARTOUM
El Obeid
White Nile
Blue Nile
ASMARA
Ras Dashen
4,620 m
Gonder
Lake Tana
DJIBOUTI
Gulf of Aden
Sheep
ndnuts
Lake Chad
NDJAMENA
Maiduguri
Cotton
Carrying
millet
Darfur
Kordofan
Oil
Ethiopian
Highlands
DJIBOUTI
Kano
ria
of
ABUJA
IGERIA
Garoua
Chari
Oil
Massif
des Bongo
Groundnuts
Hippopotamus
Sudd
Coffee
ADDIS ABABA
Great Rift Valley
Goats
Horn
of Africa
Ogaden
ETHIOPIA
Giraffe
SOMALIA
Benue
The Spiral
of Progress
CENTRAL AFRICAN
REPUBLIC
Ubangi
Diamond
mining
Dung
beetle
Gold
mining
Oil
Adamawa
Highlands
Cocoa
Cotton
YAOUNDÉ
CAMEROON
BANGUI
Gorilla
MOGADISHU
Mogadishu
Oil
EQUATORIAL
GUINEA
SÃO TOMÉ
& PRÍNCIPE
GABON
UGANDA
KENYA
Equator
Kismaayo
Somalia
Fishing
CONGO
RWANDA
BURUNDI
DEMOCRATIC
REPUBLIC
OF CONGO
Bananas
ANGOLA
(CABINDA)
TANZANIA
ANGOLA

Tunisia
Libya
Egypt
Sudan
Eritrea
Ethiopia
Djibouti
Niger
Chad
Central African
Republic

0   500   1000 km
0   250   500 miles

Central and Southern Africa

Lowland covered with lush rainforests stretches across much of the centre of Africa, although the rainforests are shrinking as trees are cut down for export. Further east are vast areas of savannah, with long grasses and scattered trees. Many of Africa's well-known wild animals live around the savannahs, and thousands of tourists visit each year to see them. A volcanic mountain range forms the borders between Rwanda, Uganda and the Democratic Republic of Congo. Bitter wars have been fought here in recent years. Further south lies a high plateau. Many of the rivers here have mighty waterfalls, such as the Victoria Falls on the borders of Zambia and Zimbabwe. These rivers are dammed for hydroelectricity. Namibia and Botswana are both dry countries with desert areas – the Namib and Kalahari. South Africa is by far the wealthiest country in Africa, with its rich gold and diamond mines.

FACTS AND FIGURES

Largest cities
Kinshasa 7,274,000
Johannesburg 3,226,000
Durban 3,090,000

Highest mountain
Kilimanjaro 5,895 m

Largest lakes
Lake Victoria 69,500 km²
Lake Tanganyika 32,900 km²

Longest river
Nile 6,695 km

Mountain high
Kilimanjaro is the highest mountain in Africa. It is made up of three separate volcanic peaks called Kibo, Mawensi and Shira. It is so high that snow covers its peaks all year.

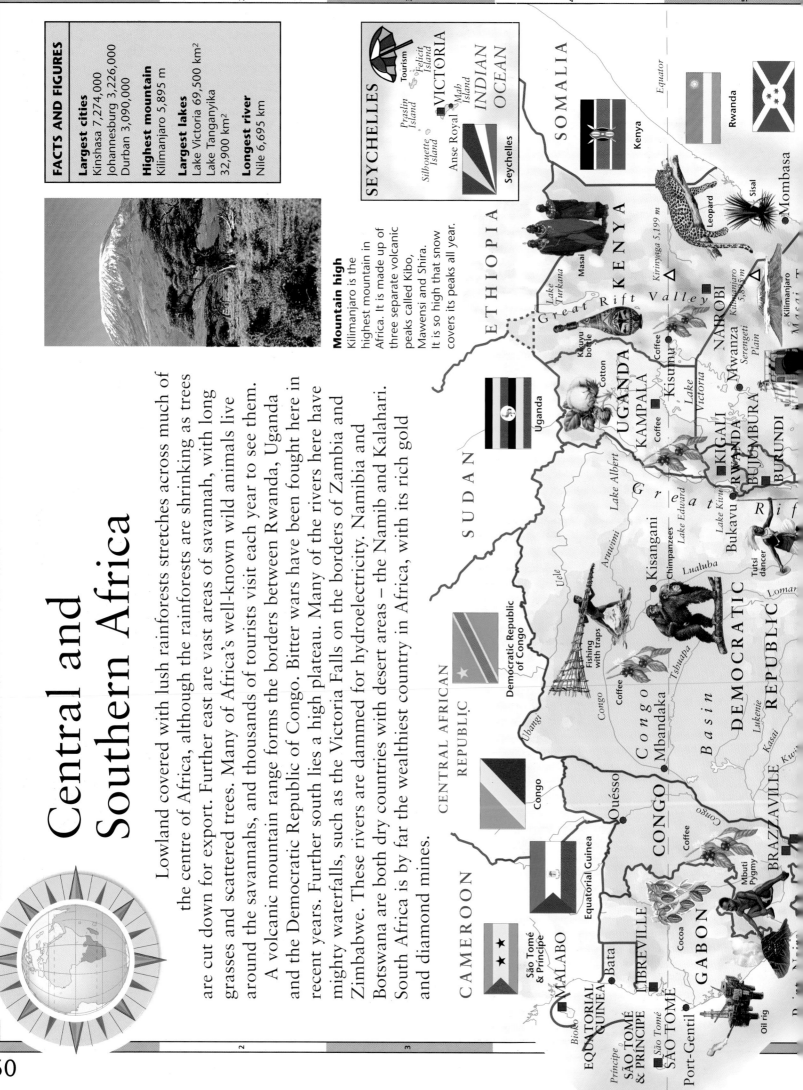

SEYCHELLES

Tourism
Praslin Island
Silhouette Island
Felicit Island
Anse Royal
Mah Island
VICTORIA
INDIAN OCEAN
Seychelles

SOMALIA

Kenya
Rwanda

ETHIOPIA

KENYA
Lake Turkana
Masai
Great Rift Valley
Kirinyaga 5,199 m
NAIROBI
Kilimanjaro 5,895 m
Mombasa
Sisal
Leopard

SUDAN

UGANDA
KAMPALA
Coffee
Cotton
Kisumu
Lake Victoria
Mwanza
Serengeti Plain

Uganda

Lake Albert
Lake Edward
Lake Kivu
KIGALI
RWANDA
Bukavu
BUJUMBURA
BURUNDI
Tutsi dancer

CENTRAL AFRICAN REPUBLIC

Democratic Republic of Congo

Great Rif

Arunwmi
Uele
Kisangani
Chimpanzees
Luluba
Lomami
DEMOCRATIC REPUBLIC
Fishing with traps
Congo
Coffee
Mbandaka
Basin
Tshuapa
Lukenie
Kasai
Lualuba
Kwi

Ubangi
Ouésso
Congo
Congo
Coffee

CONGO
BRAZZAVILLE
Coffee

CAMEROON

Equatorial Guinea
Bata
São Tomé & Príncipe
Príncipe
São Tomé
SÃO TOMÉ & PRÍNCIPE
SÃO TOMÉ
MALABO
EQUATORIAL GUINEA
Bioko
LIBREVILLE
Cocoa
GABON
Port-Gentil
Mbuti Pygmy
Oil rig

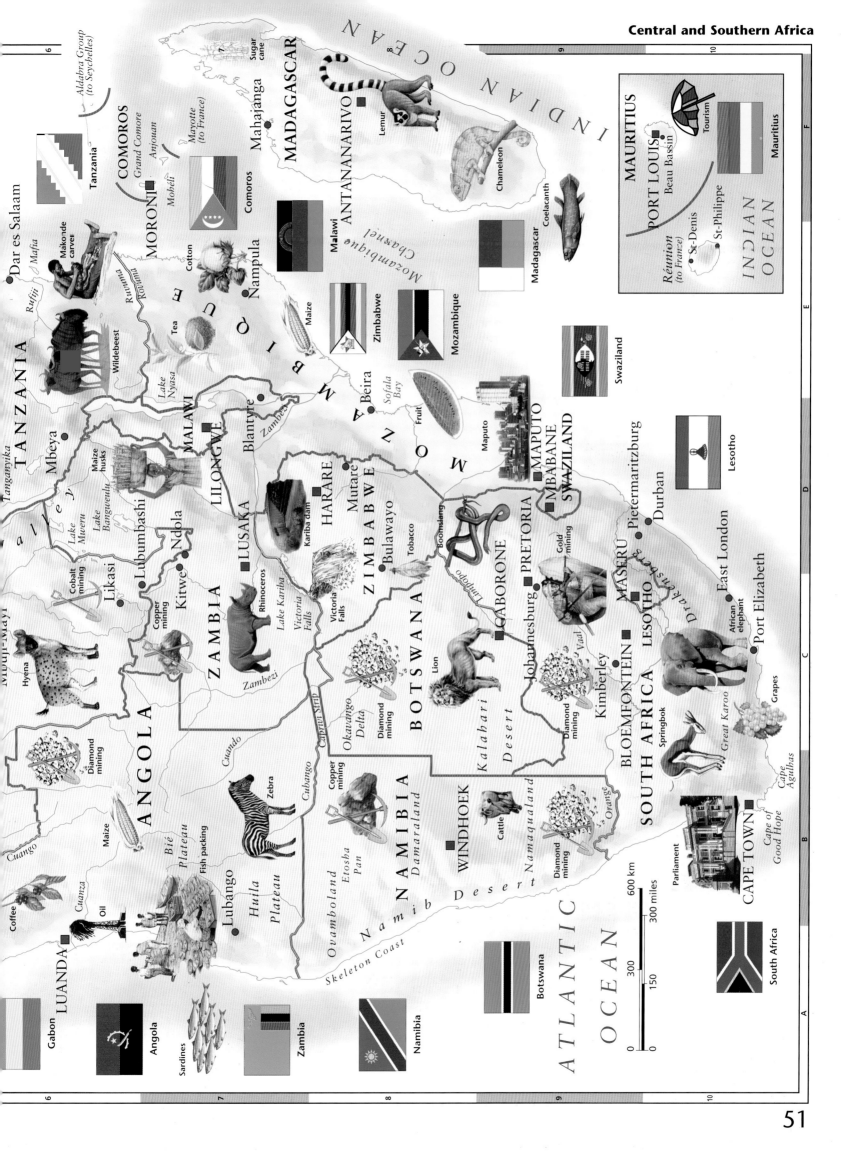

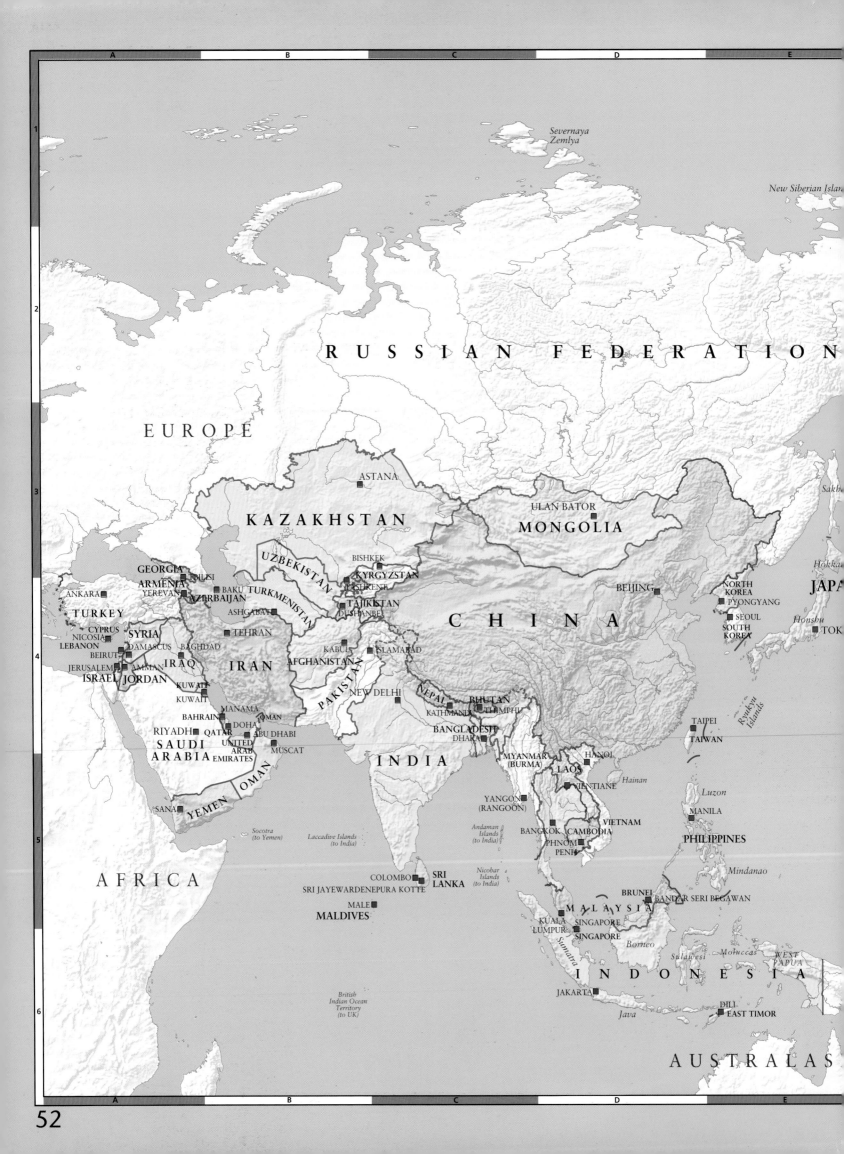

RUSSIAN FEDERATION

EUROPE

Severnaya Zemlya

New Siberian Islands

ASTANA

KAZAKHSTAN

ULAN BATOR

MONGOLIA

UZBEKISTAN

BISHKEK

GEORGIA
TBILISI
ARMENIA
YEREVAN
BAKU
AZERBAIJAN
TURKMENISTAN
KYRGYZSTAN
TASHKENT
TAJIKISTAN
DUSHANBE

BEIJING

NORTH
KOREA
PYONGYANG

JAPAN

ANKARA

ASHGABAT

CHINA

SEOUL
SOUTH
KOREA

Hokka

Honshu

TOK

TURKEY

CYPRUS
NICOSIA
LEBANON
BEIRUT
DAMASCUS
SYRIA
TEHRAN

KABUL
ISLAMABAD

Ryukyu Islands

JERUSALEM
AMMAN
ISRAEL JORDAN

BAGHDAD
IRAQ

IRAN

AFGHANISTAN

KUWAIT
KUWAIT

PAKISTAN

NEW DELHI

NEPAL
KATHMANDU

BHUTAN
THIMPHU

TAIPEI
TAIWAN

MANAMA
BAHRAIN
RIYADH
QATAR
DOHA
ABU DHABI
UNITED
ARAB
EMIRATES
OMAN
MUSCAT

BANGLADESH
DHAKA

HANOI

MYANMAR
(BURMA)
LAOS

SAUDI
ARABIA

INDIA

VIENTIANE

Hainan

Luzon

YEMEN OMAN

SANA

YANGON
(RANGOON)

MANILA

*Socotra
(to Yemen)*

*Laccadive Islands
(to India)*

*Andaman
Islands
(to India)*

BANGKOK
CAMBODIA
PHNOM
PENH

VIETNAM

PHILIPPINES

Mindanao

AFRICA

*Nicobar
Islands
(to India)*

COLOMBO
SRI
LANKA
SRI JAYEWARDENEPURA KOTTE

MALE
MALDIVES

BRUNEI
BANDAR SERI BEGAWAN

MALAYSIA
KUALA
LUMPUR
SINGAPORE
SINGAPORE

Borneo

Sulawesi
Moluccas

*WEST
PAPUA*

INDONESIA

*British
Indian Ocean
Territory
(to UK)*

JAKARTA

Sumatra

Java

DILI
EAST TIMOR

AUSTRALAS

52

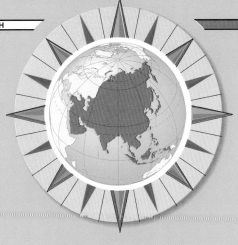

0 1000 2000 km
0 500 1000 miles

Wrangel Island

islands

ASIA

On top of the world
The Himalayas is the highest mountain range in the world. The mountains stretch for 2,400 km and snow and glaciers cover many of the peaks all year.

Asia is the largest continent. It makes up about 35 per cent of the Earth's land surface and is home to 60 per cent of the population. It stretches from Turkey and the Ural Mountains of Russia in the west to the Pacific Ocean in the east, and from the icy Arctic Ocean in the north to the tropical islands of Indonesia, with their steamy rainforests, in the south. The landscape of this vast area is varied. The world's highest mountain, Mount Everest in the Himalayas, is always covered with snow, while elsewhere, in the middle of the continent, there are huge swathes of bare, rocky desert. Frozen plains cover much of the far north. Lake Baikal, the world's deepest lake, is in Asia, together with some of the world's greatest rivers – the Yangtze and the Ganges.

Asia contains three huge and populous countries – the Russian Federation, China and India – as well as several that are not as large. It is a diverse continent, with a wide variety of peoples, beliefs, languages and lifestyles. It contains some of the world's poorest regions and wealthiest big cities.

Following Buddhism
Buddhism is one of the religions followed by millions of people in Asia. It is the most widespread religion in Myanmar and affects much of daily life there. Even children, such as this girl, can become monks or nuns.

The Russian Federation

The Russian Federation is the largest country in the world. It stretches across both Europe and Asia. Most of the people live to the west of the Ural Mountains, in the European part of the country. Large birch and conifer forests cover the region, and the River Volga brings water.

The eastern part of the Russian Federation is in Asia. This vast area includes regions of marshland and the largest coniferous forest in the world as well as the grassy plains known as steppes. Most of Russia's grain is grown on large farms there.

The Russian Federation was formed in 1991, after the earlier break-up of the communist Soviet Union. Many former states became independent countries. Under Soviet rule, industries were run by the state, and many were outdated. Today, the country is modernizing many of its industries and farming techniques.

SWEDEN

NORWAY

FINLAND

Gulf of Bothnia

Arctic Circle

Barents Sea

Murmansk

Iron ore mining

Kola Peninsula

Fishing

Kaliningrad

LATVIA

ESTONIA

RUSS. FED.

St Petersburg

White Sea

Archangel

Reindeer

Novaya Zer

Ka Se

POLAND

LITHUANIA

Lake Ladoga

Lake Onega

Northern Dvina

Pechora

Pen

BELARUS

St Basil's cathedral

Siberian tit

Hazel grouse

Gora Narodnaya 1,895 m

UKRAINE

MOSCOW

North

Nizhniy Novgorod

Kirov

Ballet

European

Ural Mountains

West

R

Kazan

Perm

Siberia

Plain

Plain

Wheat farming

Steel making

Oil

Yekaterinburg

Rostov-na-Donu

Don

Volgograd

Volga

Samara

Industry

F

E

Black Sea

Caucasus

Oil

Chelyabinsk

Ural

Elbrus 5,642 m

GEORGIA

Irtysh

Omsk

ARMENIA

Caspian Sea

Ind

AZERBAIJAN

KAZAKHSTAN

Royal homes
The Winter Palace in St Petersburg was the winter home of the tsars (the Russian royal family). It was built in 1732CE.

FACTS AND FIGURES

Largest cities
Moscow 12,500,000
St Petersburg 4,581,000

Longest river
Yenisey-Angara 5,540 km

Largest lake
Lake Baikal 30,500 km². This is the deepest freshwater lake in the world

Highest mountain
Elbrus 5,642 m. This, in the European part of Russia, is the highest point in Europe

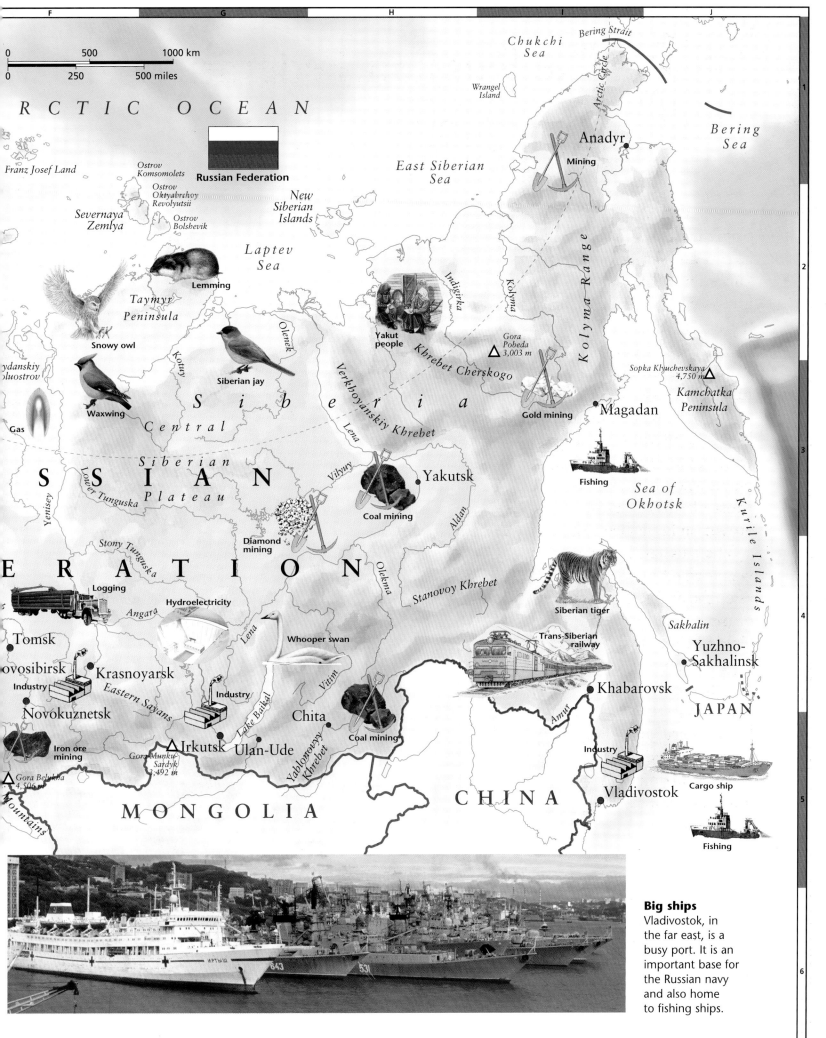

0 500 1000 km

0 250 500 miles

ARCTIC OCEAN

Russian Federation

Franz Josef Land

Ostrov Komsomolets

Ostrov Oktyabrskoy Revolyutsii

Severnaya Zemlya

Ostrov Bolshevik

New Siberian Islands

Laptev Sea

Chukchi Sea

Bering Strait

Wrangel Island

Arctic Circle

Bering Sea

East Siberian Sea

Anadyr

Mining

Lemming

Taymyr Peninsula

Snowy owl

ydanskiy oluostrov

Siberian jay

Kottuy

Olenek

S i b e r i a

Central

Waxwing

Gas

Indigirka

Kolyma

Kolyma Range

Yakut people

Khrebet Cherskogo

Gora Pobeda 3,003 m

Sopka Klyuchevskaya 4,750 m

Kamchatka Peninsula

Gold mining

Magadan

Verkhoyanskiy Khrebet

Lena

Fishing

Sea of Okhotsk

Kurile Islands

S S I A N

Lower Tunguska

Siberian Plateau

Yenisey

Vilyuy

Coal mining

Yakutsk

Diamond mining

Aldan

E R A T I O N

Stony Tunguska

Logging

Hydroelectricity

Olekma

Stanovoy Khrebet

Siberian tiger

Angara

Lena

Whooper swan

Tomsk

ovosibirsk

Krasnoyarsk

Eastern Sayans

Industry

Industry

Vitim

Trans-Siberian railway

Sakhalin

Yuzhno-Sakhalinsk

Novokuznetsk

Iron ore mining

Gora Belukha 4,506 m

Gora Munku-Sardyk 3,492 m

Irkutsk

Lake Baikal

Ulan-Ude

Chita

Yablonovyy Khrebet

Coal mining

Amur

Khabarovsk

Industry

Vladivostok

Cargo ship

JAPAN

Mountains

MONGOLIA

CHINA

Fishing

Big ships
Vladivostok, in the far east, is a busy port. It is an important base for the Russian navy and also home to fishing ships.

West Asia

Three continents – Europe, Asia and Africa – all meet in West Asia, which is also known as the Middle East. It is the only place on earth where this happens, and the region has long been used by traders. The world's first cities grew up in the area between the rivers Tigris and Euphrates, about 5,500 years ago.

West Asia's northern borders are made up of mountains and seas. To the west is the Mediterranean Sea, while further south are the warm waters of the Red Sea, The Gulf and the Indian Ocean. The rivers Tigris and Euphrates bring fertility to the lands that surround them, but most of West Asia is desert or semi-desert with a climate that is mostly hot and dry. Saudi Arabia's 'Empty Quarter' is one of the most inhospitable areas on earth.

Three of the world's most widespread religions – Judaism, Christianity and Islam – have their roots in West Asia. Oil and natural gas have brought great wealth to many countries, and the region produces over one-third of the world's daily oil output. Unfortunately, both oil and religion have led to bitter conflicts. There are border disputes within Israel, which was founded in 1948 from an area called Palestine, and has been torn by conflict ever since. Thousands of Palestinians have been displaced, and want to set up their own country in their ancient homelands. Fighting continues in many parts of the region and the area is politically unsettled.

FACTS AND FIGURES

Largest cities
Tehran 11,850,000
Istanbul 10,019,000
Baghdad 5,750,000

Longest river
Euphrates 2,700 km

Highest mountain
Qolleh ye Damavand 5,618 m

Oldest city
Damascus, the capital of Syria, is the world's oldest continuously inhabited city, at around 4,500 years old

A place to worship
Istanbul is one of Turkey's most attractive cities. Islam is the national religion, and the city has many beautiful mosques, such as the Suleymaniye Mosque, shown.

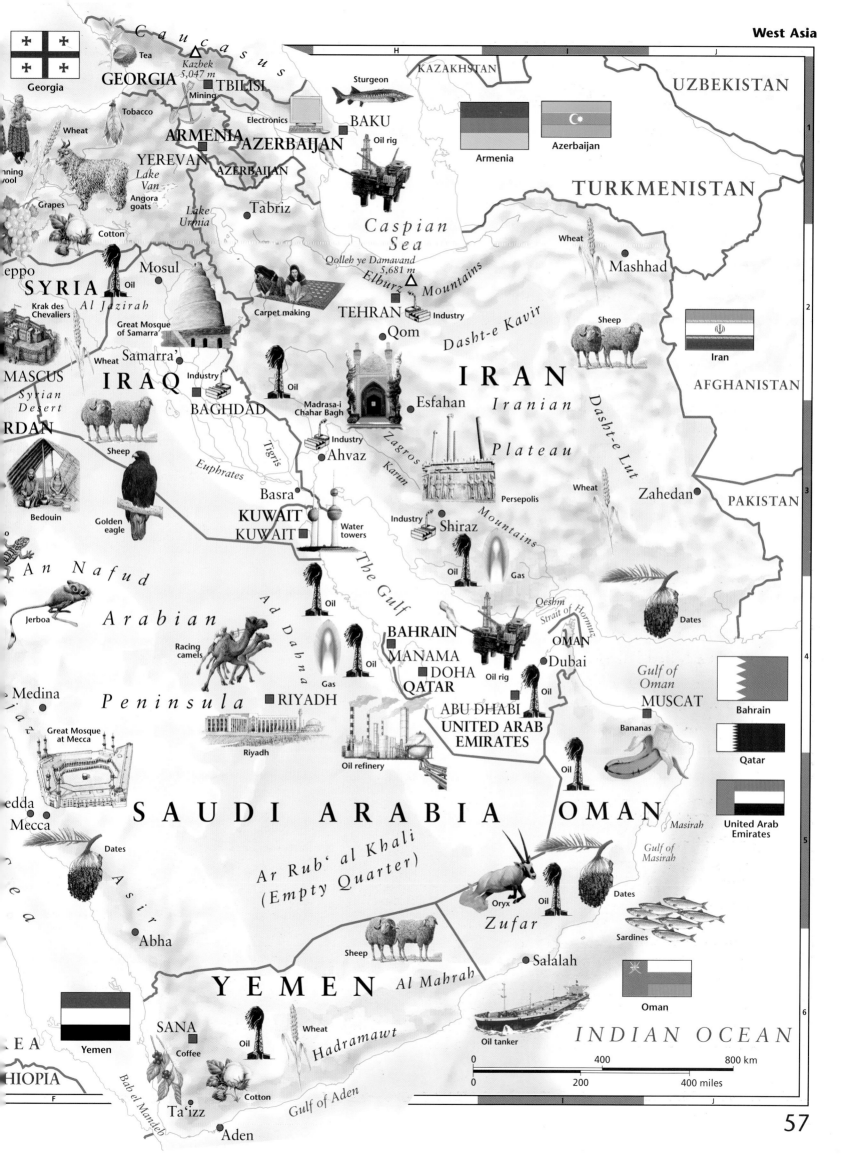

Georgia

Caucasus

Kazbek 5,047 m

GEORGIA

TBILISI

Mining

Tea

KAZAKHSTAN

UZBEKISTAN

Tobacco

Wheat

Electronics

Sturgeon

BAKU

Oil rig

TURKMENISTAN

ARMENIA

AZERBAIJAN

YEREVAN

AZERBAIJAN

Lake Van

Angora goats

Lake Urmia

Tabriz

Caspian Sea

Qolleh ye Damavand 5,681 m

Wheat

Mashhad

Armenia

Azerbaijan

Grapes

Cotton

ning wool

Mosul

SYRIA

Oil

Al Jazirah

Great Mosque of Samarra'

Carpet making

Elburz Mountains

TEHRAN

Industry

Qom

Dasht-e Kavir

Sheep

Iran

AFGHANISTAN

eppo

Krak des Chevaliers

MASCUS

Wheat

Samarra'

IRAQ

Syrian Desert

RDAN

Sheep

Bedouin

Golden eagle

Industry

BAGHDAD

Madrasa-i Chahar Bagh

Oil

Industry

Ahvaz

Zagros

Karun

IRAN

Esfahan

Iranian Plateau

Industry

Persepolis

Wheat

Dasht-e Lut

Zahedan

PAKISTAN

An Nafud

Jerboa

Arabian

Euphrates

Tigris

Basra

KUWAIT

KUWAIT

Water towers

Ad Dahna

Racing camels

Shiraz

Mountains

Oil

Gas

Qeshm

Strait of Hormuz

Dates

Peninsula

Oil

Gas

BAHRAIN

MANAMA

DOHA

QATAR

Oil

Oil rig

OMAN

Dubai

Gulf of Oman

MUSCAT

Bahrain

Medina

Great Mosque at Mecca

RIYADH

ABU DHABI

UNITED ARAB EMIRATES

Bananas

Qatar

edda

Mecca

Riyadh

Oil refinery

Oil

United Arab Emirates

Dates

Asir

SAUDI ARABIA

OMAN

Masirah

EA

Abha

Ar Rub' al Khali (Empty Quarter)

Zufar

Oryx

Oil

Dates

Gulf of Masirah

Sardines

HIOPIA

Sheep

Al Mahrah

Salalah

Oman

YEMEN

SANA

Wheat

Hadramawt

Oil tanker

INDIAN OCEAN

Oil

Coffee

Yemen

0   400   800 km

0   200   400 miles

Bab el Mandeb

Cotton

Ta'izz

Gulf of Aden

Aden

Central Asia

Much of Central Asia is mountainous, with fertile plains and rocky deserts. The world's second highest mountain, K2, is found there, in the Karakoram mountain range in Pakistan. Highlands make up much of Afghanistan and have an effect on the climate there. Northerly winds bring cold winters, but summers are hot and dry. Many of the countries in central Asia are landlocked (surrounded by other countries, with no coasts); because they are so far from the sea, their climates tend to be dry with little rainfall. Kazakhstan has cold, snowy winters with warm summers.

There are many freshwater lakes in the region, and water from these is used to irrigate crops. However, this can cause problems – so much water has been taken from the Amu and Syr rivers in Uzbekistan that the Aral Sea is drying out.

The mighty Indus river flows through Pakistan. Its waters support life along the fertile plains. In southwestern Pakistan, there are large areas of desert. Throughout history, the lands of Pakistan have been invaded and controlled by various other nations. Peaceful settlers have also made their homes here, and the population reflects this racial mix.

Traditional lifestyles

Millions of Afghans live a nomadic way of life, tending small flocks of goats and sheep. They live in felt-lined tents called yurts, which can be packed up and moved around easily.

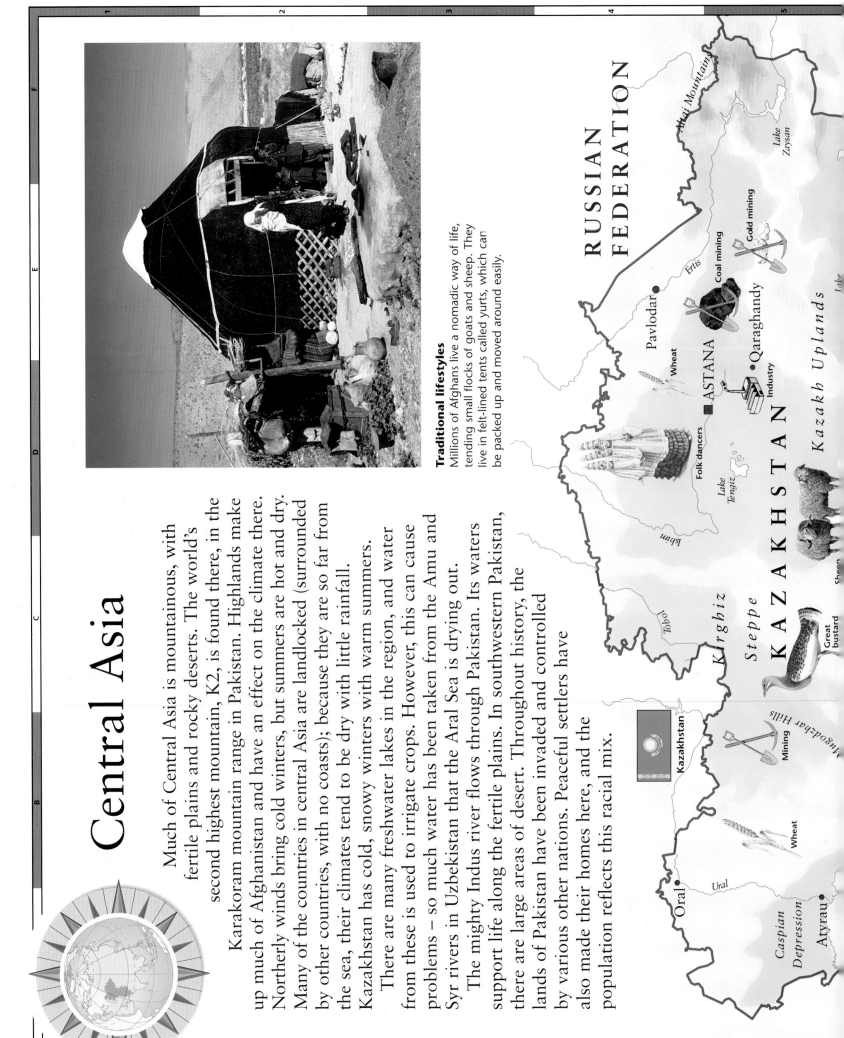

RUSSIAN FEDERATION

Altai Mountains

Lake Zaysan

KAZAKHSTAN

Kazakh Uplands

Steppe

Kirghiz

Caspian Depression

Mugodzhar Hills

Oral

Ural

Atyrau

Tobol

Lake Tengiz

Ishim

Irtis

Pavlodar

Wheat

ASTANA

Qaraghandy

Industry

Coal mining

Gold mining

Folk dancers

Wheat

Mining

Great bustard

Sheep

Lake

Kazakhstan

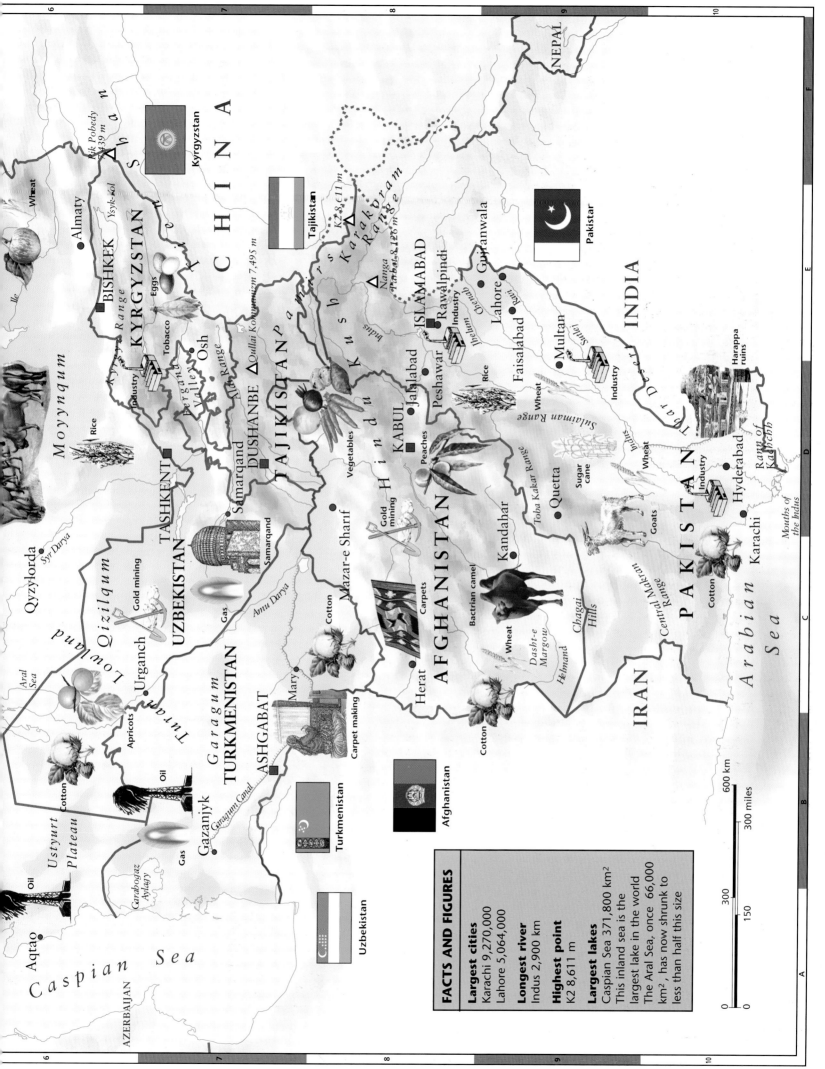

Kyrgyzstan

Tajikistan

Pakistan

Wheat

Ïk Pobedy
439 m

Ysyk-köl

K2 8,611 m

NEPAL

Almaty

T i e n   S h a n

BISHKEK

C H I N A

Eggs

Tobacco

KYRGYZSTAN

Kyrgyz Range

Osh

Alai Range

Fergana Valley

P a m i r s

Karakoram Range

Nanga Parbat, 8,126 m

ISLAMABAD

Gujranwala

INDIA

Industry

Rice

Industry

Qullai Kommunizm 7,495 m

Rawalpindi

Lahore

Moyynqum

Samarqand

DUSHANBE

TAJIKISTAN

H i n d u   K u s h

Peshawar

Jhelum

Chenab

Ravi

Faisalabad

Multan

Industry

Harappa ruins

Ile

Rice

Vegetables

KABUL

Jalalabad

Sutlej

T h a r   D e s e r t

Syr Darya

TASHKENT

Samarqand

Gold mining

Mazar-e Sharif

Peaches

Rice

Sulaiman Range

Qyzylorda

UZBEKISTAN

Q i z i l q u m

Gold mining

Amu Darya

Gold mining

AFGHANISTAN

Kandahar

Quetta

Sugar cane

Wheat

Industry

Hyderabad

Rann of Kachchh

T u r a n   L o w l a n d

Gas

Carpets

Bactrian camel

Toba Kakar Range

Goats

Mouths of the Indus

Aral Sea

Urganch

Cotton

GARAGUM

TURKMENISTAN

Cotton

Herat

Wheat

Dasht-e Margow

Helmand

Chagai Hills

Central Makran Range

P A K I S T A N

Cotton

Karachi

A r a b i a n   S e a

Apricots

Amu Darya

Mary

Carpet making

IRAN

Ustyurt Plateau

Cotton

ASHGABAT

Garagum Canal

Turkmenistan

Afghanistan

Oil

Gazanjyk

Gas

Uzbekistan

Aqtao

Oil

Garabogaz Aylagy

C a s p i a n   S e a

AZERBAIJAN

600 km

300 miles

300

150

0   0

FACTS AND FIGURES

Largest cities
Karachi 9,270,000
Lahore 5,064,000

Longest river
Indus 2,900 km

Highest point
K2 8,611 m

Largest lakes
Caspian Sea 371,800 km² This inland sea is the largest lake in the world The Aral Sea, once 66,000 km², has now shrunk to less than half this size

South Asia

South Asia is bordered by the Thar Desert to the northwest and the Himalayas, a great chain of towering mountains, in the north and east. The Himalayas contain some of the highest mountains in the world, including the highest of all, Mount Everest. They are so high that they are covered with snow all year round, and most of the people of Bhutan and Nepal live in the more sheltered valleys to the south.

In Bangladesh, by contrast, most of the land is low-lying and flat. The mighty Ganges and Brahmaputra rivers flow through fertile valleys into the sea. Every year, monsoon rains swell these rivers and can cause terrible floods.

Much of India is covered with rolling plateau land, where farmers grow corn and millet and graze their animals. Over 60 per cent of the country's vast population makes its living from agriculture, but the country is also home to large-scale industries and huge, crowded cities.

Sri Lanka is a mountainous island off the southern coast of India. It is fringed with beautiful beaches. Inland is a fertile plain, which is an important tea-growing area.

Religious river

The Ganges is a sacred river to followers of the Hindu religion. They make pilgrimages to the river to bathe in its cleansing waters. Steps, or ghats, have been built at points along its banks to help people get in and out of the water.

Map labels

PAKISTAN

CHINA

NEPAL
KATHMANDU
Dhaulagiri 8,167 m
Mount Everest 8,848 m

BHUTAN
THIMPHU
Kula Kangri 7,554 m
Bhutan

BANGLADESH

Nepal

Jammu and Kashmir
Srinagar
Aksai Chin (administered by China, claimed by India)
(administered by China, claimed by India)
Demchok (administered by China, claimed by India)

Indus
Amritsar
Golden Temple at Amritsar
Golden eagle

Himalaya
Siwalik Range
Yamuna
Ganges
Ghaghara
Lucknow
Varanasi
Kanpur
Industry
Wheat

Delhi
Industry
NEW DELHI
Computers
Jaipur
Chambal
Agra
Taj Mahal
Gandhi

Leopard
Bengal tiger
Peacock

Thar Desert
Aravali Range

Indian elephant
Naga Hills
Brahmaputra
Indian rhinoceros
Jute

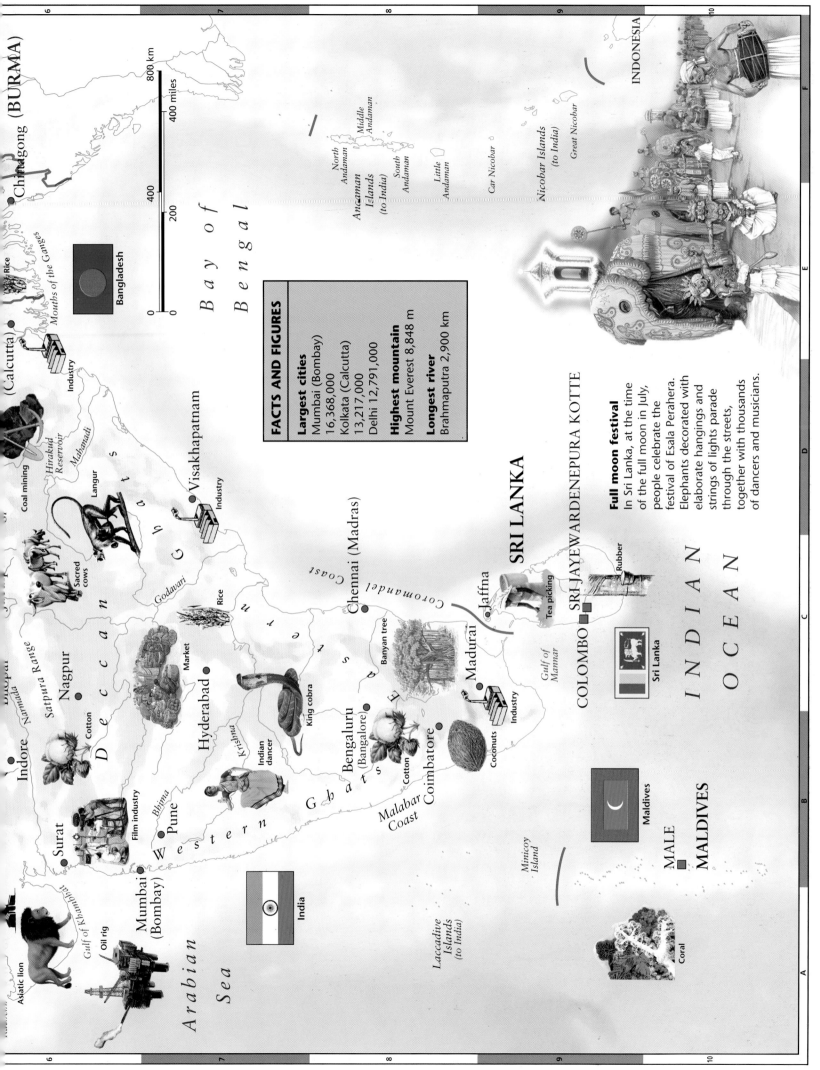

Chittagong (BURMA)

Rice

Mouths of the Ganges

(Calcutta)

Industry

Bangladesh

800 km

400 miles

400

200

0

B a y   o f

B e n g a l

North Andaman

Middle Andaman

Andaman Islands (to India)

South Andaman

Little Andaman

Car Nicobar

Nicobar Islands (to India)

Great Nicobar

INDONESIA

FACTS AND FIGURES

Largest cities
Mumbai (Bombay)
16,368,000
Kolkata (Calcutta)
13,217,000
Delhi 12,791,000

Highest mountain
Mount Everest 8,848 m

Longest river
Brahmaputra 2,900 km

Coal mining

Hirakud Reservoir

Mahanadi

Langur

Sacred cows

Visakhapatnam

Industry

Godavari

Rice

D e c c a n

Nagpur

Cotton

Market

Hyderabad

Krishna

King cobra

Indian dancer

Chennai (Madras)

Banyan tree

Coromandel Coast

Eastern Ghats

Jaffna

SRI LANKA

SRI JAYEWARDENEPURA KOTTE

Rubber

Tea picking

COLOMBO

Sri Lanka

Gulf of Mannar

Bengaluru (Bangalore)

Cotton

Madurai

Industry

Coconuts

I N D I A N

O C E A N

Full moon festival

In Sri Lanka, at the time
of the full moon in July,
people celebrate the
festival of Esala Perahera.
Elephants decorated with
elaborate hangings and
strings of lights parade
through the streets,
together with thousands
of dancers and musicians.

Indore

Narmada

Satpura Range

Western Ghats

Bhima

Pune

Film industry

Coimbatore

Malabar Coast

Minicoy Island

Maldives

MALE

MALDIVES

Surat

Gulf of Khambhat

Oil rig

Mumbai (Bombay)

India

Laccadive Islands (to India)

Coral

A r a b i a n

S e a

Asiatic lion

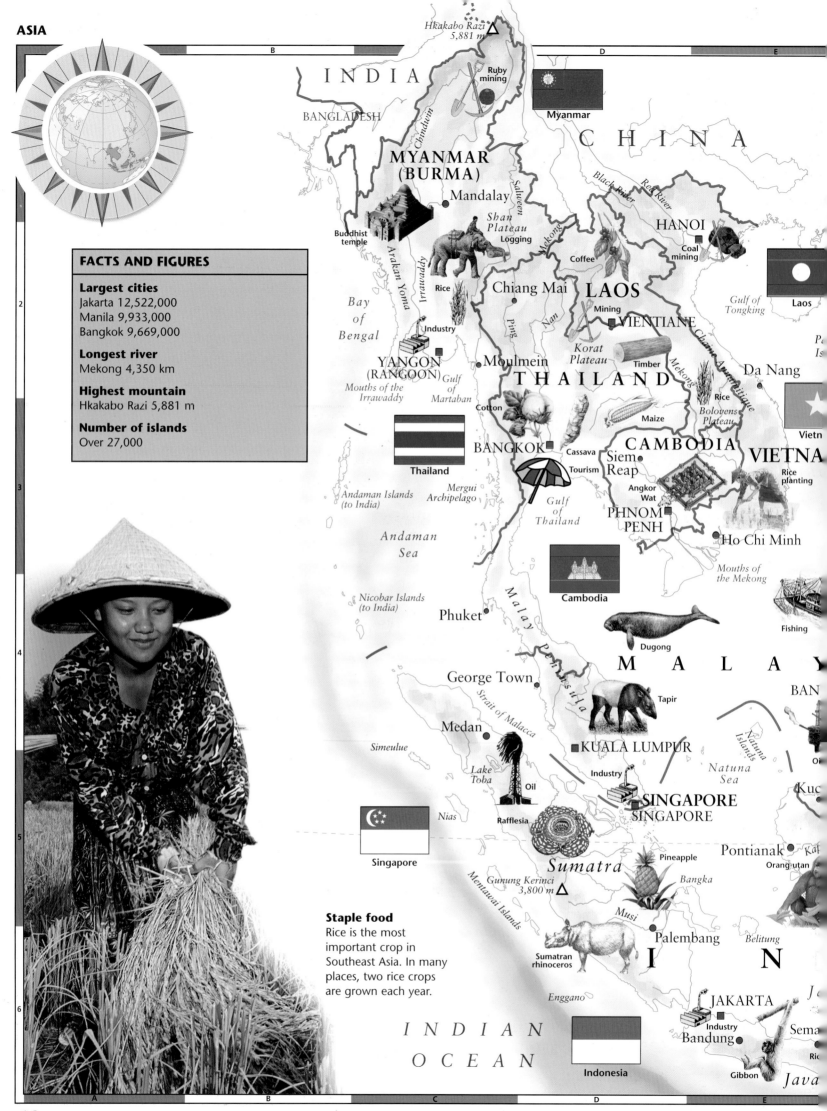

FACTS AND FIGURES

Largest cities
Jakarta 12,522,000
Manila 9,933,000
Bangkok 9,669,000

Longest river
Mekong 4,350 km

Highest mountain
Hkakabo Razi 5,881 m

Number of islands
Over 27,000

Hkakabo Razi
5,881 m

INDIA

BANGLADESH

Ruby mining

Myanmar

CHINA

MYANMAR
(BURMA)

Mandalay

Chindwin

Salween

Shan
Plateau

Logging

Black River

Red River

HANOI

Coal
mining

Buddhist
temple

Arakan Yoma

Irrawaddy

Rice

Bay
of
Bengal

Chiang Mai

Coffee

LAOS

Gulf of
Tongking

Laos

Mekong

Ping

Nan

Mining

VIENTIANE

Korat
Plateau

Chaine Annamitique

Da Nang

Industry

YANGON
(RANGOON)

Moulmein

THAILAND

Timber

Mekong

Rice

Pe
Is

Mouths of the
Irrawaddy

Gulf
of
Martaban

Cotton

Maize

Bolovens
Plateau

Vietn

BANGKOK

Cassava

Siem
Reap

CAMBODIA

VIETNA

Thailand

Tourism

Angkor
Wat

Rice
planting

Andaman Islands
(to India)

Mergui
Archipelago

Gulf
of
Thailand

PHNOM
PENH

Ho Chi Minh

Andaman
Sea

Cambodia

Mouths of
the Mekong

Nicobar Islands
(to India)

Phuket

Malay Peninsula

Dugong

Fishing

George Town

MALAY

Strait of Malacca

Tapir

BAN

Medan

Natuna
Islands

Simeulue

KUALA LUMPUR

Natuna
Sea

Oi

Lake
Toba

Oil

Industry

SINGAPORE
SINGAPORE

Kuč

Nias

Singapore

Pontianak

Kal

Rafflesia

Sumatra

Pineapple

Bangka

Orang-utan

Singapore

Gunung Kerinci
3,800 m

Musi

Staple food
Rice is the most
important crop in
Southeast Asia. In many
places, two rice crops
are grown each year.

Enggano

Sumatran
rhinoceros

Palembang

Belitung

I

N

JAKARTA

Ja

INDIAN

Industry

Bandung

Sema

Indonesia

Ric

OCEAN

Gibbon

Java

Southeast Asia

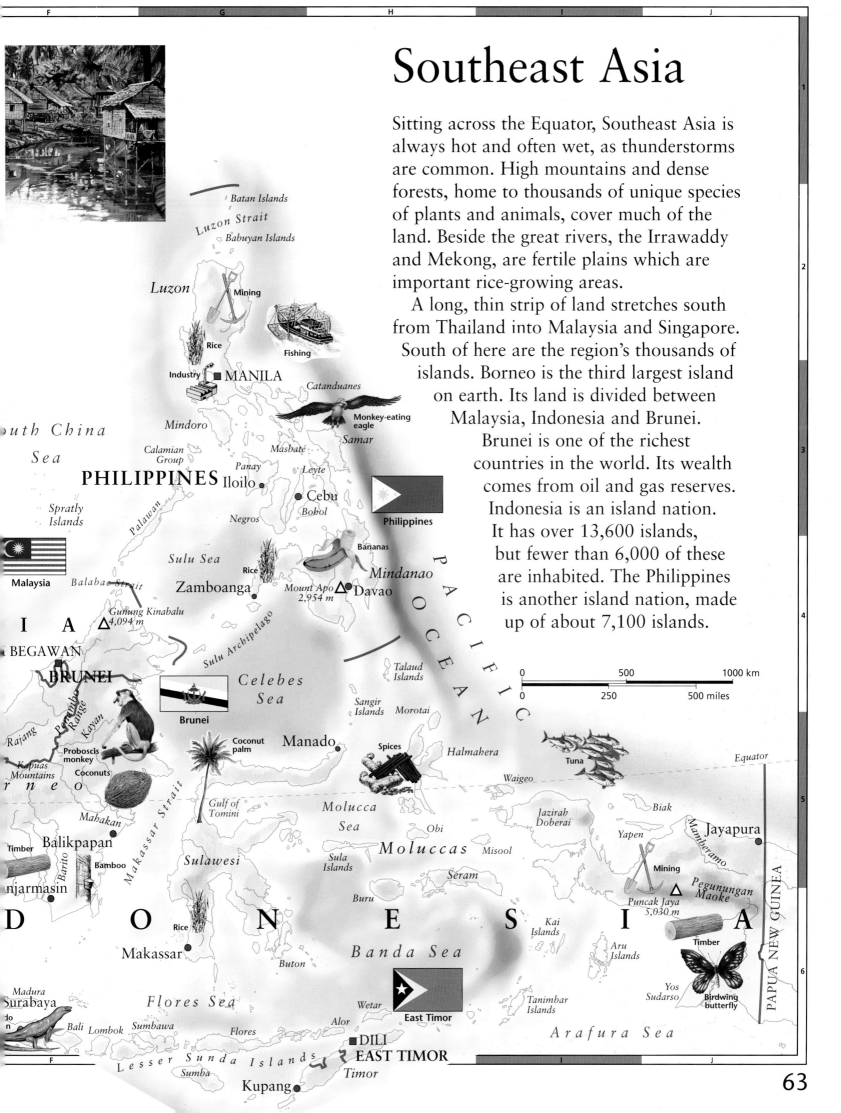

Sitting across the Equator, Southeast Asia is always hot and often wet, as thunderstorms are common. High mountains and dense forests, home to thousands of unique species of plants and animals, cover much of the land. Beside the great rivers, the Irrawaddy and Mekong, are fertile plains which are important rice-growing areas.

A long, thin strip of land stretches south from Thailand into Malaysia and Singapore. South of here are the region's thousands of islands. Borneo is the third largest island on earth. Its land is divided between Malaysia, Indonesia and Brunei. Brunei is one of the richest countries in the world. Its wealth comes from oil and gas reserves. Indonesia is an island nation. It has over 13,600 islands, but fewer than 6,000 of these are inhabited. The Philippines is another island nation, made up of about 7,100 islands.

Batan Islands

Luzon Strait

Babuyan Islands

Luzon

Mining

Rice

Fishing

Industry ■ MANILA

Catanduanes

South China Sea

Mindoro

Monkey-eating eagle

Samar

Masbate

Calamian Group

Panay

Leyte

PHILIPPINES Iloilo

Spratly Islands

Cebu

Bohol

Negros

Philippines

Malaysia

Palawan

Sulu Sea

Rice

Bananas

Mindanao

Balabac Strait

Zamboanga

Mount Apo 2,954 m

Davao

Gunung Kinabalu 4,094 m

Sulu Archipelago

I A

BEGAWAN

BRUNEI

Celebes Sea

Talaud Islands

0 500 1000 km

0 250 500 miles

Kayan

Proboscis monkey

Brunei

Coconut palm

Manado

Sangir Islands

Morotai

Spices

Halmahera

Tuna

Equator

Rajang

Kapuas Mountains

Coconuts

r n e o

Mahakan

Makassar Strait

Gulf of Tomini

Molucca Sea

Obi

Waigeo

Jazirah Doberai

Biak

Yapen

Mamberamo

Jayapura

Timber

Balikpapan

Bamboo

Sulawesi

Sula Islands

Moluccas

Misool

Seram

Mining

Pegunungan Maoke

njarmasin

Barito

D I O N E S I A

Rice

Buru

Kai Islands

Puncak Jaya 5,030 m

Timber

Makassar

Buton

Banda Sea

Aru Islands

Yos Sudarso

Birdwing butterfly

Madura

Surabaya

Bali *Lombok* *Sumbawa*

Flores Sea

Wetar

Alor

East Timor

Flores

Tanimbar Islands

Arafura Sea

PAPUA NEW GUINEA

■ DILI

EAST TIMOR

Lesser Sunda Islands

Sumba

Timor

Kupang

East Asia

China fills most of East Asia. It is the fourth largest country in the world and has the greatest population – a fifth of the world's people live there. Great rivers, such as the Yellow river and Yangtze, flow across the fertile plains. Most of China's industrial cities, as well as the farming regions, are to be found in the plains, since the mountain and desert regions are so inhospitable. The rugged mountains in the southwest are home to the giant panda, which feeds on the bamboo that grows there. In the north lies the Gobi Desert, which crosses the border into Mongolia.

Hong Kong, a major financial centre, was returned to Chinese rule in 1997.

Taiwan is a mountainous country. Most of its people live in the west of the island.

FACTS AND FIGURES

Largest cities
Shanghai 9,838,000
Beijing 7,441,000
Hong Kong 6,708,000

Longest river
Yangtze 6,300 km

Highest mountain
Everest 8,848 m. This is the highest mountain in the world

Gobi Desert temperatures
Highest 45°C; lowest -40°C

R U

Olgiy

Altai Mountain

KAZAKHSTAN

Oil

Junggar Basin

Wheat

Urumqi

KYRGYZSTAN

UZBEKISTAN

Tien Shan

Tomur Feng 7,439 m

Turpan Basin -154 m

Tarim He

Tarim Basin

TAJIKISTAN

Kashi

Lop Nur

AFGHANISTAN

Takla Makan Desert

K2 8,611 m

PAKISTAN
(administered by China, claimed by India)

Aksai Chin (administered by China, claimed by India)

Kunlun Mountains

Qai

Himalayan griffon vulture

Musk deer

Demchok (administered by China, claimed by India)

Bobak marmot

Plateau of Tibet

C

Yak

Red panda

Nu Jiang

Siberian ibex

Potala Palace

Himalayan black bear

Brahmaputra

Lhasa

NEPAL

Xixabangma Feng 8,013 m

Mount Everest 8,848 m

BHUTAN

Snow leopard

I N D I A

Keep out!
At nearly 3,460 km long, the Great Wall of China is the world's largest man-made structure. It was built to stop nomadic tribes invading China.

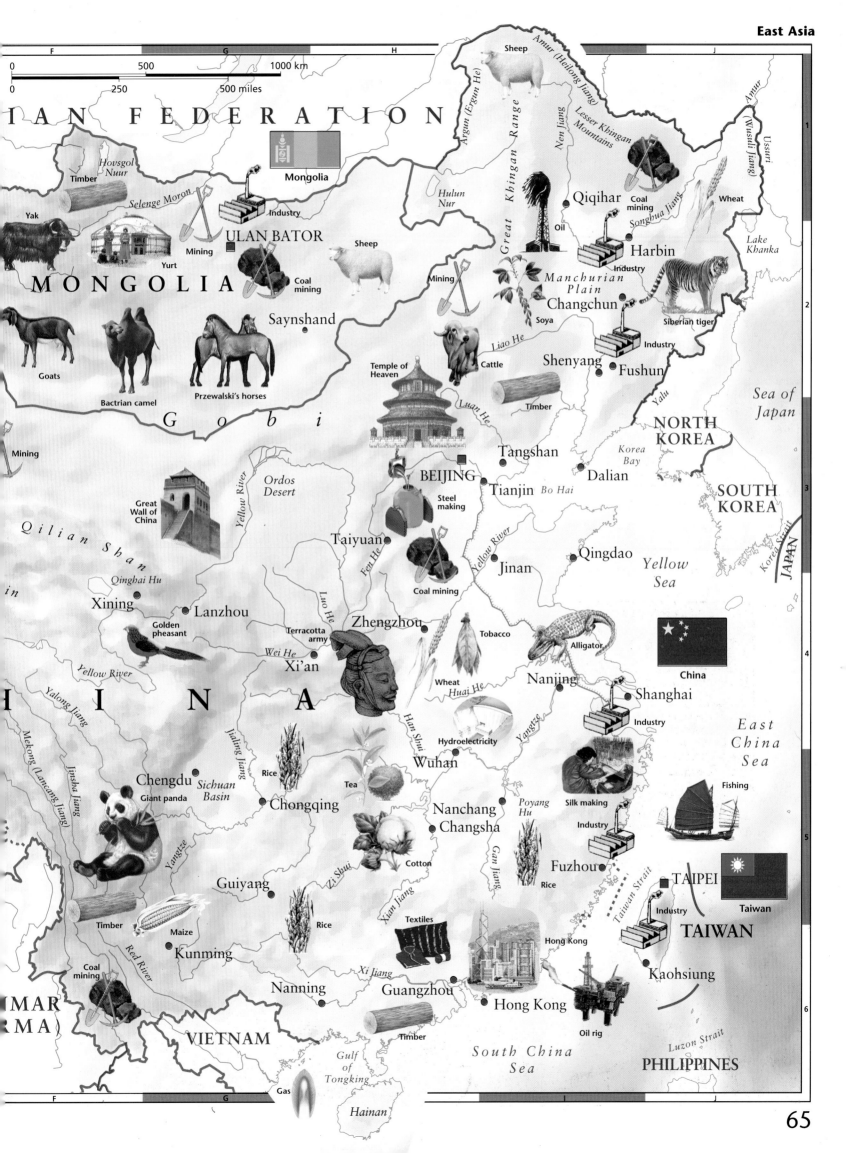

0   500   1000 km

0   250   500 miles

IAN   F E D E R A T I O N

Sheep

Amur (Heilong Jiang)

Argun (Ergun He)

Nen Jiang

Lesser Khingan Mountains

Songhua Jiang

Amur (Wusuli Jiang)

Ussuri

Hovsgol Nuur

Timber

Yak

Selenge Moron

Mongolia

Industry

Great Khingan Range

Hulun Nur

Oil

Qiqihar

Coal mining

Wheat

Lake Khanka

Mining

ULAN BATOR

Sheep

Harbin

Industry

M O N G O L I A

Coal mining

Mining

Manchurian Plain

Changchun

Soya

Siberian tiger

Goats

Saynshand

Cattle

Liao He

Shenyang

Industry

Yalu

NORTH KOREA

Fushun

Sea of Japan

Bactrian camel

Przewalski's horses

G o b i

Temple of Heaven

Luan He

Timber

Tangshan

Dalian

Korea Bay

SOUTH KOREA

Mining

Great Wall of China

Yellow River

Ordos Desert

BEIJING

Steel making

Tianjin

Bo Hai

Q i l i a n   S h a n

Qinghai Hu

Taiyuan

Coal mining

Yellow River

Jinan

Qingdao

Yellow Sea

JAPAN

Korea Strait

Xining

Lanzhou

Golden pheasant

Yellow River

Zhengzhou

Tobacco

Alligator

China

Terracotta army

Wei He

Xi'an

Wheat

Huai He

Nanjing

Shanghai

Industry

East China Sea

H I N A

Yalong Jiang

Jinsha Jiang

Mekong (Lancang Jiang)

Jialing Jiang

Rice

Han Shui

Hydroelectricity

Wuhan

Yangtze

Silk making

Industry

Fishing

Chengdu

Sichuan Basin

Giant panda

Tea

Nanchang

Changsha

Poyang Hu

Industry

Chongqing

Yangtze

Cotton

Gan Jiang

Fuzhou

Rice

TAIPEI

Industry

Taiwan

Guiyang

Zi Shui

Rice

Textiles

Hong Kong

TAIWAN

Timber

Maize

Kunming

Red River

Coal mining

Xi Jiang

Guangzhou

Hong Kong

Kaohsiung

MAR RMA)

VIETNAM

Nanning

Oil rig

Luzon Strait

Gas

Gulf of Tongking

South China Sea

PHILIPPINES

Hainan

65

Japan and the Koreas

The islands of Japan are mountainous and rugged. About 3,000 islands form a long chain along the Pacific coast of Asia. The largest and most populated islands are Honshu, Hokkaido, Kyushu and Shikoku. Japan is in an earthquake zone and many of the islands are active volcanoes. Buildings need to be able to withstand tremors. The highest of the volcanoes is Mount Fuji, which last erupted in 1707CE.

Most of the people of Japan live in bustling cities along the coasts. But Japanese people also love nature, and celebrate it in many festivals and ceremonies. In the north of the country the climate is mainly cool, with snow in the winters. Further south, it is milder with hot, humid summers and fierce storms called typhoons in September.

North Korea and South Korea are part of a peninsula of land that stretches into the Sea of Japan. Mountains cover much of both countries. Along the coasts are plains, where most of the people live. Both North and South Korea have cold, snowy winters. The summers are usually hot and wet.

North Korea trades little with other countries, whereas South Korea, like Japan, exports goods all over the world.

Ritual contest
Traditional martial arts are popular in Japan and the Koreas. Kendo, shown here, is a form of fencing that has its origins in the training of the samurai, the warriors of ancient Japan.

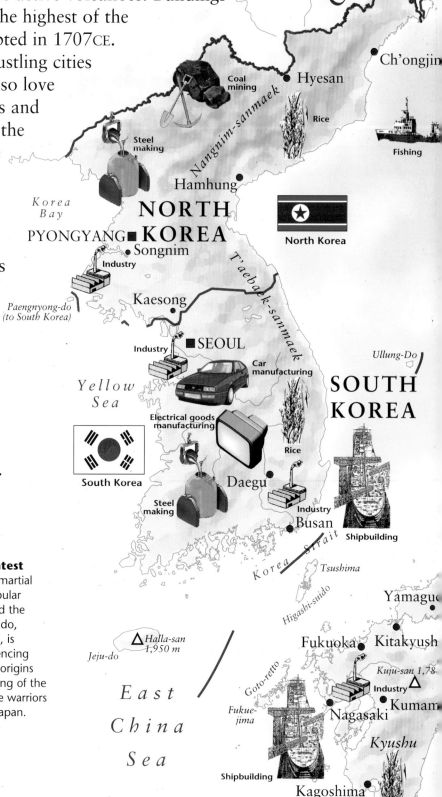

CHINA

Ch'ongjin

Coal mining

Hyesan

Nangnim-sanmaek

Rice

Fishing

Steel making

Hamhung

Korea Bay

NORTH

PYONGYANG■ **KOREA**

North Korea

● Songnim

Industry

T'aebaek-sanmaek

Paengnyong-do (to South Korea)

Kaesong

■SEOUL

Industry

Car manufacturing

Ullung-Do

SOUTH KOREA

Yellow Sea

Electrical goods manufacturing

Rice

South Korea

Daegu

Steel making

Industry

Busan

Shipbuilding

Korea Strait

Tsushima

Higashi-suido

Yamagu

△Halla-san 1,950 m

Jeju-do

East China Sea

Fukuoka

Kitakyush

Kuju-san 1,78

Goto-retto

Industry

△

Fukue-jima

Nagasaki

Kumam

Kyushu

Shipbuilding

Kagoshima

Rice

Sata-misaki

Ryukyu Islands

Yaku-shima

Tanega-sh

La Perouse Strait

Soya-misaki

Rebun-to

Rishiri-to

RUSSIAN FEDERATION

Kurile Islands (administered by Russian Federation)

Macaque

Shiretoko-misaki

0   200   400 km
0   100   200 miles

Industry

Asahikawa

△ *Asahi-dake* 2,290 m

Kussharo-ko

Hokkaido

Car manufacturing

Sapporo

Kushiro

Rice

FACTS AND FIGURES

Largest cities
Tokyo 36,760,000
This is the largest city in the world
Seoul 21,300,000
Osaka 17,520,000

Number of earthquakes
Between 800 and 1,000 each year

Number of volcanoes
Japan has over 200 volcanoes. Most are extinct (not able to erupt), but 77 are considered active (able to erupt)

Highest mountain
Mount Fuji 3,776 m

Okushiri-to

Uchiura-wan

Factory fishing

Hakodate

Fishing

Tsugaru-kaikyo

Shimokita-hanto

Mutsu-wan

Sardines

Aomori

Hachinohe

Apples

Fishing

Akita

Silka deer

Fishing

Time for tea
Each aspect of the Japanese tea ceremony is full of meaning. This ritual way of preparing and drinking tea is influenced by Zen Buddhism.

Fishing

Rice

Sado-shima

Sendai

Sendai-wan

Niigata

Fukushima

S e a   o f

J a p a n

Japan

Honshu

Industry

Noto-hanto

Computers

Hitachi

Toyama-wan

JAPAN

Kanazawa

Toyama

Nagano

Cameras

Tea

Dogo

Oki-shoto

zen

Cherry blossom

Funabashi

Himeji castle

Wakasa-wan

TOKYO

Kawasaki

Chiba

Giant salamander

Gifu

△ *Mount Fuji* 3,776 m

Yokohama

Biwa-ko

Nagoya

Industry

Okayama

Kyoto   Nara

Nojima-zaki

Kobe

Motorcycle manufacturing

Sakai   Osaka

Hamamatsu

Industry

Iroshima

Ise-wan

Tuna

Sagami-nada

I z u - s h o t o

n d   S e a

atsuyama

Kii-suido

Bullet train

ikoku

Citrus fruit

Fishing

Tosa-wan

Muroto-zaki

Shiono-misaki

PACIFIC

OCEAN

suido

Fishing

PACIFIC

OCEAN

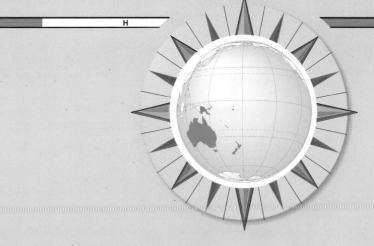

F   G   H   J

WAII
(US)

waii
0   1000   2000 km
0   500   1000 miles

Marquesas
Islands

Tuamotu Islands

Society Islands

Tahiti

French
Polynesia
(to France)

Gambier
Islands

Pitcairn
Island   Pitcairn
Islands
(to UK)

1

2

3

4

AUSTRALASIA & OCEANIA

Australasia & Oceania is made up of the great land mass of Australia and many thousands of islands in the Pacific Ocean. Australia itself is one of the seven continents. Many of the Pacific islands were formed by underwater volcanic eruptions. Coral reefs often grow around these islands. Tropical storms, called typhoons, regularly batter these islands, and the area is also prone to tsunamis – huge waves caused by underwater volcanoes or earthquakes.

Fourteen countries make up Australasia & Oceania: Australia, New Zealand, Papua New Guinea and several island nations which have become independent in the last 20 years. The rest of the islands are dependencies of other countries.

Flower power
Lush plants and flowers grow in the tropical Cook Islands, and these girls have made traditional garlands called leis.

Island hopping
Of the 330 islands that make up Fiji, only 106 are inhabited. Scattered throughout the rest of the region are over 20,000 small islands, and much larger ones including Australia and New Zealand.

F   G   H

Australia

Australia is the world's largest island. Its land is mostly flat, with the main highland area being the Great Dividing Range in the east of the country. To the west are semi-arid plains where only scrub and grasses grow. Much of Western Australia is desert. In the far north, there are lush rainforests and mangrove swamps.

Despite its huge size, only about 20 million people live in Australia. Most of them live in towns and cities along the south and east coasts. The first people in Australia were the Aborigines, but the population is now made up mainly of people who migrated to Australia from Europe, from the 18th century CE onwards.

Australia is home to many animals that are not found anywhere else on earth. These include marsupials (mammals that carry their young in pouches), such as kangaroos, wombats and koalas.

FACTS AND FIGURES

Largest cities
Sydney 4,119,000
Melbourne 3,593,000
Brisbane 1,763,000

Longest river
Murray-Darling 3,750 km

Largest lake
Lake Eyre 9,100 km². This lake varies in size throughout the year

Highest mountain
Mount Kosciuszko 2,230 m

Famous skyline
Sydney's harbour is one of the greatest in the world. The magnificent Harbour Bridge spans the channel dividing north and south Sydney. This bridge and the Opera House are recognized all over the world.

Timor Sea

Cape Londonderry

Bonaparte Archipelago

Wyndha[m]

Kings Sound

Cape Lévêque

Kimberle[y]

Plateau

Derby

INDIAN OCEAN

Fitzroy

Flying doctor

Striped possum

Eighty Mile Beach

Great Sandy Desert

Road train

Dingo

Exmouth Gulf

North West Cape

Ashburton

Hamersley Range

Lake Disappointment

Newman

A U

Gibson Desert

Oil rig

Lake Macleod

WESTERN

Iron ore mining

Lake Carnegie

Kangaroo

Echidna

Carnarvon

AUSTRALIA

Shark Bay
Dirk Hartog Island

Sheep farm

Emu

Lake Barlee

Lake Carey

Great Victo[ria] Desert

Geraldton

Gold mining

Lake Moore

Kalgoorlie

Boulder

Industry

Lake Cowan

Nullar[bor]

Perth
Fremantle

Wheat farming

Fishing

Cape Pasley

Sheep

Great white shark

Cape Leeuwin

Albany

New Zealand

New Zealand is made up of two large islands and several smaller ones. Much of the land is volcanic and there are many active volcanoes including Mount Ngaurahoe and Mount Ruapehu on North Island. Hot springs, pools of boiling mud, and geysers are common, particularly around Rotorua, and steam from these is used to produce electricity. South Island is dominated by the Southern Alps, which stretch down the western side of the island and are home to the country's highest mountain, Mount Cook, and the Franz Josef and Fox glaciers.

New Zealand's fertile lands provide rich pasture for millions of sheep and cattle. In fact, there are more sheep than people living there!

The first people to live in New Zealand were the Maori – settlers from Polynesia. Throughout the 19th century CE, Europeans began to move there, and they now make up about 90 per cent of the population. Most people live in the cities and coastal towns.

North Cape
Great Exhibition Bay
Ninety Mile Beach
Sheep
Rugby
Industry
Kaipara Harbour
Great Barrier Island
Hauraki Gulf
Auckland
Manukau Harbour
Coromandel Peninsula
Steel making
Waikato
Bay of Plenty
Hamilton
Kiwi fruit
North Island
Lake Rotorua
Wheat
Rotorua
Sheep shearing
Lake Taupo
Possum
Dairy cattle
North Taranaki Bight
Mount Egmont (Taranaki) 2,518 m
Mount Ngaurahoe 2,291 m
Mount Ruapehu 2,797 m
Cape Egmont
Wanganui
Hawke Bay
Mahia Peninsu
South Taranaki Bight
Kiwi
Sheep
Tasman Sea
Cape Farewell
D'Urville Island
Golden Bay
Tasman Bay
Cook Strait
Tourism
Industry
Karamea Bight
Possum
New Zealand
Cape Foulwind
Maori art
Wellington
WELLINGTON
Cape Palliser
South Island
Southern Alps
Sheep
Kaikoura
Industry
Tourism
Sperm whale
NEW ZEALAND
Franz Josef glacier
Tuatara
Pegasus Bay
Kiwi
Mount Cook 3,754 m
Lake Tekapo
Canterbury Plains
Christchurch
Banks Peninsula
Lake Ellesmere
PACIFIC OCEAN
Cascade Point
Mount Aspiring 3,030 m
Lake Wanaka
Lake Hawea
Wheat
Canterbury Bight
Fishing
Lake Wakatipu
Yellow-eyed penguin
Tourism
Lake Te Anau
Queenstown
Roxburgh
Industry
Fiordland
Resolution Island
West Cape
Possum
Sheep
Waiau
Clutha
Mataura
Hydroelectric dam
Dunedin
Otago Peninsula
Albatross
Dolphin
Foveaux Strait
Seal
South West Cape
Stewart Island

FACTS AND FIGURES

Largest cities
Auckland 1,208,000
Wellington 398,000
Christchurch 361,000

Longest river
Waikato 425 km

Largest lake
Lake Taupo over 600 km^2

Highest mountain
Mount Cook 3,754 m

0   100   200 km
0   50   100 miles

The Poles
The Arctic

The northernmost and southernmost points on earth are called the poles. Each pole is bitterly cold and is surrounded by huge ice sheets. The North Pole floats on an ice sheet in the Arctic Ocean. The Arctic itself is an area that includes the North Pole, the Arctic Ocean and the most northerly parts of North America, Europe and Asia. During the short summers, the Arctic ice sheet shrinks, but in winter, when temperatures can fall as low as -60°C, the ice sheet grows again. Many people live in the lands of the cold Arctic, including the Inuit, Saami and Yugyt. It is also home to polar bears, caribou and walruses.

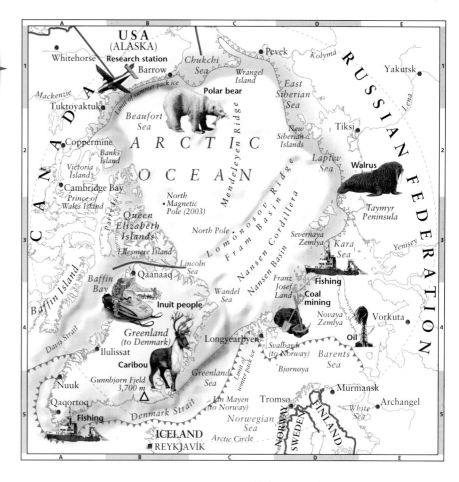

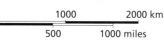

Antarctica

The South Pole is in Antarctica, which is the fifth largest of the seven continents. Except for a few sheltered dry valleys in the mountains the vast land mass is covered by snow and ice. Antarctica is the windiest place on earth and endures some of the coldest temperatures. Huge chunks of ice sometimes break off the ice sheets and form icebergs. These float in the water with 90 per cent of their bulk hidden beneath the waves, posing a danger to ships. There are no countries in Antarctica, and the only people who live there are teams of scientists who work at over 70 research stations that have been set up there.

FACTS AND FIGURES

COUNTRIES AND CAPITALS:
NORTH AMERICA

Antigua & Barbuda	St John's
Bahamas	Nassau
Barbados	Bridgetown
Belize	Belmopan
Canada	Ottawa
Costa Rica	San José
Cuba	Havana
Dominica	Roseau
Dominican Republic	Santo Domingo
El Salvador	San Salvador
Grenada	St George's
Guatemala	Guatemala City
Haiti	Port-au-Prince
Honduras	Tegucigalpa
Jamaica	Kingston
Mexico	Mexico City
Nicaragua	Managua
Panama	Panama City
St Kitts & Nevis	Basseterre
St Lucia	Castries
St Vincent & the Grenadines	Kingstown
Trinidad & Tobago	Port of Spain
United States of America	Washington D.C.

COUNTRIES AND CAPITALS:
SOUTH AMERICA

Argentina	Buenos Aires
Bolivia	La Paz and Sucre
Brazil	Brasília
Chile	Santiago
Colombia	Bogotá
Ecuador	Quito
Guyana	Georgetown
Paraguay	Asunción
Peru	Lima
Surinam	Paramaribo
Uruguay	Montevideo
Venezuela	Caracas

COUNTRIES AND CAPITALS:
EUROPE

Albania	Tirana
Andorra	Andorra la Vella
Austria	Vienna
Belarus	Minsk
Belgium	Brussels
Bosnia & Herzegovina	Sarajevo
Bulgaria	Sofia
Croatia	Zagreb
Czech Republic	Prague
Denmark	Copenhagen
Estonia	Tallinn
Finland	Helsinki
France	Paris
Germany	Berlin
Greece	Athens
Hungary	Budapest
Iceland	Reykjavik
Italy	Rome
Latvia	Riga
Liechtenstein	Vaduz
Lithuania	Vilnius
Luxembourg	Luxembourg
Macedonia	Skopje
Malta	Valletta
Moldova	Chisinau
Monaco	Monaco
Montenegro	Podgorica
Netherlands	Amsterdam and The Hague
Norway	Oslo
Poland	Warsaw
Portugal	Lisbon
Republic of Ireland	Dublin
Romania	Bucharest
Russian Federation	Moscow
San Marino	San Marino
Serbia	Belgrade
Slovakia	Bratislava
Slovenia	Ljubljana
Spain	Madrid
Sweden	Stockholm
Switzerland	Bern
Ukraine	Kiev
United Kingdom	London
Vatican City	Vatican City

COUNTRIES AND CAPITALS:
AFRICA

Algeria	Algiers
Angola	Luanda
Benin	Porto-Novo
Botswana	Gaborone
Burkina Faso	Ouagadougou
Burundi	Bujumbura
Cameroon	Yaoundé
Cape Verde	Praia
Central African Republic	Bangui
Chad	Ndjamena
Comoros	Moroni
Congo	Brazzaville
Democratic Republic of Congo	Kinshasa
Djibouti	Djibouti
Egypt	Cairo
Equatorial Guinea	Malabo
Eritrea	Asmara
Ethiopia	Addis Ababa
Gabon	Libreville
Gambia	Banjul
Ghana	Accra
Guinea	Conakry
Guinea-Bissau	Bissau
Ivory Coast	Yamoussoukro
Kenya	Nairobi
Lesotho	Maseru
Liberia	Monrovia
Libya	Tripoli
Madagascar	Antananarivo
Malawi	Lilongwe
Mali	Bamako
Mauritania	Nouakchott
Mauritius	Port Louis
Morocco	Rabat
Mozambique	Maputo
Namibia	Windhoek
Niger	Niamey
Nigeria	Abuja
Rwanda	Kigali
São Tomé & Príncipe	São Tomé
Senegal	Dakar
Seychelles	Victoria
Sierra Leone	Freetown
Somalia	Mogadishu

South Africa	Pretoria, Bloemfontein and Cape Town
Sudan	Khartoum
Swaziland	Mbabane
Tanzania	Dodoma
Togo	Lomé
Tunisia	Tunis
Uganda	Kampala
Zambia	Lusaka
Zimbabwe	Harare

COUNTRIES AND CAPITALS:

ASIA

Afghanistan	Kabul
Armenia	Yerevan
Azerbaijan	Baku
Bahrain	Manama
Bangladesh	Dhaka
Bhutan	Thimphu
Brunei	Bandar Seri Begawan
Cambodia	Phnom Penh
China	Beijing
Cyprus	Nicosia
East Timor	Dili
Georgia	Tbilisi
India	New Delhi
Indonesia	Jakarta
Iran	Tehran
Iraq	Baghdad
Israel	Jerusalem

(Jerusalem is not recognized by the international community as Israel's capital. Nearly all countries treat another city, Tel Aviv, as Israel's capital.)

Japan	Tokyo
Jordan	Amman
Kazakhstan	Astana
Kuwait	Kuwait
Kyrgyzstan	Bishkek
Laos	Vientiane
Lebanon	Beirut
Malaysia	Kuala Lumpur
Maldives	Male

Mongolia	Ulan Bator
Myanmar (Burma)	Yangon (Rangoon)
Nepal	Kathmandu
North Korea	Pyongyang
Oman	Muscat
Pakistan	Islamabad
Philippines	Manila
Qatar	Doha
Russian Federation	Moscow
Saudi Arabia	Riyadh
Singapore	Singapore
South Korea	Seoul
Sri Lanka	Colombo and Sri Jaywardenepura Kotte
Syria	Damascus
Taiwan	Taipei
Tajikistan	Dushanbe
Thailand	Bangkok
Turkey	Ankara
Turkmenistan	Ashgabat
United Arab Emirates	Abu Dhabi
Uzbekistan	Tashkent
Vietnam	Hanoi
Yemen	Sana

COUNTRIES AND CAPITALS:

AUSTRALASIA AND OCEANIA

Australia	Canberra
Fiji Islands	Suva
Kiribati	Bairiki
Marshall Islands	Majuro
Micronesia	Palikir
Nauru	no capital
New Zealand	Wellington
Palau	Melekeok
Papua New Guinea	Port Moresby
Samoa	Apia
Solomon Islands	Honiara
Tonga	Nuku'alofa
Tuvalu	Fongafale
Vanuatu	Port-Vila

LONGEST RIVERS

Nile, Africa	6,670 km
Amazon, South America	6,448 km
Yanqtze, Asia	6,300 km
Mississippi-Missouri, North America	6,020 km
Yenisey-Angara, Asia	5,540 km
Yellow River, Asia	5,464 km
Ob-Irtysh, Asia	5,409 km
Paraná-Rio de la Plata, South America	4,880 km
Congo, Africa	4,700 km
Lena, Asia	4,400 km

HIGHEST MOUNTAINS

Asia: Mount Everest	8,848 m
South America: Aconcagua	6,960 m
North America: Mount McKinley	6,194 m
Africa: Mount Kilimanjaro	5,895 m
Europe: Mount Elbrus	5,642 m
Antarctica:, Vinson Massif	4,897 m
Australasia (Australia and New Zealand) Mount Cook	3,754 m

LARGEST LAKES

Caspian Sea, Asia-Europe	371,800 km²
Superior, North America	82,350 km²
Victoria, Africa	69,500 km²
Huron, North America	59,600 km²
Michigan, North America	57,800 km²
Tanganyika, Africa	32,900 km²
Great Bear, North America	31,800 km²
Baikal, Asia	30,500 km²
Malawi/Nyasa, Africa	29,600 km²
Great Slave, North America	28,500 km²

The Aral Sea in Asia, once about 66,000 km², is rapidly shrinking

Index

This index lists all the town and city names and some of the major physical features on the maps in this atlas. For a city or town, the index gives the name and the country in which it is found. For entries that are not cities or towns, there is a word in italics describing the kind of feature it is. You will find physical features listed under their proper name rather than their description. For example, Mount Etna appears as 'Etna, Mount' in the index.

Each entry gives the number of the page on which the place or feature is found. The letter and figure after the page number give the grid square.

Acknowledgements

The publisher would like to thank the following for permission to reproduce their material. Every care has been taken to trace copyright holders. However, if there have been unintentional omissions or failure to trace copyright holders, we apologize and will, if informed, endeavour to make corrections in any future edition.

Key: b = bottom, c = centre, l = left, r = right, t = top

2tr George H. H. Huey/Corbis; 2br Getty Images; 3tl Robin Smith/Getty Images; 3tr Frans Lemmens/Getty Images; 3bl Torleif Svensson/Corbis; 3cr Australian Picture Library/Corbis; 4bl Alison Wright/Corbis; 4bcl Randy Wells/Corbis; 4bcr Galen Rowell/Corbis; 4br Bob Krist/Corbis; 4–5tc Image State/Alamy; 5bl Getty Images; 11tl Nathan Benn/Corbis; 11cl Darwin Wiggett/Corbis; 11br Brooke Slezak/Getty Images; 13 David Stoecklein/Corbis; 16 Joseph Sohm; Visions of America/Corbis; 19 Danny Lehman/Corbis; 21 Don Herbert/Getty Images; 23tl Will & Deni McIntyre/ Getty Images; 23bl Jerry Alexander/Getty Images; 23br Travel Pix/Getty Images; 24bl Getty Images; 27 Hubert Stadler/Corbis; 28–29bc John Lamb/Getty Images; 28br Connie Coleman/Getty Images; 31 Dallas and John Heaton/ Corbis; 32 Getty Images; 34 Doug Armand/Getty Images; 37 Getty Images; 39 Buddy Mays/Corbis; 41 Peter Adams/Getty Images; 43 ML Sinibaldi/ Corbis; 44 Michael Freeman/Corbis; 46–47tc Wolfgang Kaehler/Corbis; 47cl Tibor Bognár/Corbis; 47br Angelo Cavalli/Getty Images; 48 Nik Wheeler/Corbis; 50 Torleif Svensson/Corbis; 53bl Craig Lovell/Corbis; 53br Peter Adams/Getty Images; 55 Wolfgang Kaehler/Corbis; 56 Fergus O'Brien/ Getty Images; 58 Robert Harding Picture Library Ltd/Alamy; 60 Frans Lemmens/Getty Images; 62 Jochem D. Wijnands; 64 Getty Images; 67 Frank Leather; Eye Ubiquitous/Corbis; 68–69 Peter Adams/Getty Images; 69br Nicholas DeVore/Getty Images; 70 Australian Picture Library/Corbis; 74 V.C.L./Getty Images; Back cover br Travel Pix/Getty Images.